"Ben Walton has written an excellent guide to preaching Old Testament narratives. Well versed in biblical hermeneutics and homiletics, he offers an insightful, practical, step-by-step method, illustrated with many examples, for preaching Old Testament narratives relevantly. I highly recommend this book to those who wish to preach Old Testament narratives with divine authority."
**Sidney Greidanus, Professor of Preaching Emeritus,
Calvin Theological Seminary**

"Pastors around the globe desiring to preach all of God's word faithfully will find Benjamin Walton's book *Preaching Old Testament Narratives* to be extremely helpful. Walton guides the preacher throughout the entire process of studying and proclaiming the Old Testament narratives. This book is quite readable and yet very thorough, addressing all of the important issues that preachers encounter in proclaiming the Old Testament stories. This is an outstanding work, a valuable tool that seasoned pastors and beginning pastors alike will want to read, study, and employ in their preaching."
J. Daniel Hays, Professor of Biblical Studies, Ouachita Baptist University

"Read this book before you preach from any biblical narrative and it will skillfully steer you away from some common mistakes and toward very constructive alternatives. More than that, its short chapters and accessible style will help you improve, among other things, introductions, conclusions, and how you preach Christ. Take up and read!"
**Greg R. Scharf, Chair of Pastoral Theology and Professor of Homiletics,
Trinity Evangelical Divinity School**

"The narratives of the Old Testament present a technical challenge for the preacher. But in the end, they are still just stories that compel attention even as they offer truth. Ben Walton helps us navigate these technical aspects without losing the heart of these stories. This book draws from deep reserves of homiletic wisdom. If we listen to this wisdom, we just might help our people deeper into the heart of God."
**Kenton C. Anderson, Professor of Homiletics, ACTS Seminaries of
Trinity Western University, President, Northwest Baptist Seminary**

"Most Christians know only a limited number of the Old Testament's narratives, largely because so few pastors have the confidence to preach them. Ben Walton helpfully addresses this problem, showing how these narratives continue to be relevant for Christians today and how they can be preached authentically. Preachers will find clear guidance, both in the processes of interpreting these narratives and also in the steps to developing interesting sermons on them."
**David G. Firth, Old Testament Tutor, Head of Research,
St. John School of Mission (Nottingham, UK)**

"Ben Walton has given us a gift in this wonderful summary of a sound hermeneutical approach to the Scriptures. Paul admonished us to 'rightly divide the word of truth,' and with this tool in hand any student of the Bible, if they have the discipline, will be able to be 'a workman who need not be ashamed.'"
Darryl DelHousaye, President, Phoenix Seminary

"A welcome, thorough guide for pastors brave enough to preach on Old Testament narratives—and to further sharpen their skills. A full menu of practical help and examples awaits them in this book."
Robert L. Hubbard Jr., Professor of Biblical Literature Emeritus, North Park Theological Seminary

"The narratives of the Old Testament may be at once the easiest and the most demanding passages in the Bible for preachers—easiest, because they are vivid accounts filled with arresting details that easily hold an audience's interest; demanding, because it's difficult to preach them well, in the sense of getting their theological substance right and communicating their relevance effectively. This is where Ben Walton's *Preaching Old Testament Narratives* can help. Preachers who are intent on doing justice to the stories of the Old Testament will profit greatly from Walton's counsel on how to navigate the exegetical and homiletical challenges these marvelous passages pose."
Duane Litfin, President Emeritus, Wheaton College

"As children many of us were raised on wonderful stories from the Old Testament, but it is rare indeed to hear faithful and relevant exposition of those narratives in today's pulpits. Benjamin Walton's volume, *Preaching Old Testament Narratives*, offers the sort of clear guidance necessary for all who are serious about discovering and delivering the message of the Old Testament to the church in our age. Walton's work guides the preacher through a series of practical steps and clear illustrations designed to result in messages that are rooted deeply in stories of old while turning toward the Christ who makes all things new. I recommend it highly."
Jason Hiles, Dean, College of Theology, Grand Canyon University

"Preaching from Old Testament narrative texts can be tricky for beginning preachers and seasoned expositors alike. For many listeners today, Old Testament stories may sound archaic at best, and irrelevant at worst. In this very practical and helpful resource, Ben Walton moves adeptly from hermeneutics to homiletics and offers preachers a blueprint for how to faithfully communicate God's redemptive story from Old Testament narrative passages. Read it and you will acquire concrete tips for making this important genre of Scripture come alive and find new pathways for application in your listeners' lives."
Matthew D. Kim, Assistant Professor of Preaching and Ministry, Gordon-Conwell Theological Seminary

"Springing from the homiletical and theological world of Haddon Robinson and Donald Sunukjian, this book on preaching Old Testament narrative makes its own, fresh contribution. Ben Walton writes with precision and clarity, and his thoughtful method will go a long way toward encouraging more fine sermons on the rich narrative literature of the Old Testament."
Thomas G. Long, Bandy Professor of Preaching Emeritus, Candler School of Theology, Emory University

"In his encounter with an Ethiopian court official who was reading a passage from the scroll of Isaiah, Philip began at that passage and proclaimed Jesus to the official (Acts 8: 26–35). All who teach and proclaim the gospel should be able to do the same with Old Testament narratives. Ben Walton's book will help that to happen. *Preaching Old Testament Narratives* is unique in approach and practical in design. Examined and tested by groups of pastors prior to publication, the book gives understandable guidance on narrative interpretation and helpful steps on sermon development from text selection to formulation of the take-home truth. Organized in two main parts, Discover the Message and Deliver the Message, *Preaching Old Testament Narratives* is not just a quality textbook for personal study or for a course of study; it is a complete course in a textbook, and I highly recommend it as a vital resource for those who preach and teach Old Testament narratives."
Jerry N. Barlow, Professor of Preaching and Pastoral Work, New Orleans Baptist Theological Seminary

"Ben Walton honors the Old Testament's narratives by resisting the reductionist tendency to strip them down to bottom-line principles that will rarely do justice to the divinely inspired text. *Preaching Old Testament Narratives* is a wise, well-conceived book that is very accessible and overflows with practical instruction. Those who take to heart and practice the rubrics and advice provided here will preach the narratives with fresh Spirit-infused, Christ-centered power."
R. Kent Hughes, Visiting Professor of Practical Theology, Westminster Theological Seminary

"I've always believed that God's Word is the greatest storybook of all time. While a comprehensive guide to theology and doctrine, its stories highlight the reality of God's work in human lives in colorful and dramatic ways. But preaching the narratives can often be challenging. *Preaching Old Testament Narratives* by Ben Walton will be a great guide to anyone who wants the stories of the Old Testament to come to life in their preaching without wavering from the true meaning of the text or over-spiritualizing the narrative. All of us who love telling the stories of Scripture will be grateful for Walton's contribution."
Joe Stowell, President, Cornerstone University

"For a while now I have been looking for an up-to-date book that would enable my homiletics students to grapple with and grasp how to preach from the Old Testament. Here is the answer to my prayers. Since narratives make up so much of the Old Testament, this book will certainly be a great resource. Any homiletics student—and indeed any preacher—who makes his way through this book will find his preaching true to Scripture and powerfully applied to his hearers."

**Conrad Mbewe, Chancellor, African Christian University,
Principal, Lusaka Ministerial College**

"Pastors who have been trained to preach based on Pauline texts are often challenged when facing the task of preaching those fascinating stories found in the Old Testament. So pastors will welcome Ben Walton's new book *Preaching Old Testament Narratives* as a helpful source of exegetical and homiletical insights. Walton walks us through the process, from selecting and analyzing a narrative text to shaping and then delivering such a message. The book is packed with valuable preaching ideas and tools. This volume will be a welcome addition to many a preacher's bookshelf."

**Michael Duduit,
Dean, College of Christian Studies and Clamp Divinity School,
Anderson University**

"Everybody loves a story! Perhaps that's why God put so many of them in the Bible, especially in the Old Testament. Of course, these stories took place long, long ago in places far, far away. So how do we discover their message and their relevance for modern readers? How do those of us who preach and teach communicate effectively the relevance of these ancient stories to a modern audience? If, like me, you're still thinking through answers to these questions, you need to read Benjamin Walton's *Preaching Old Testament Narratives*. In this readable, insightful book Walton provides a clear, practical, and well-illustrated guide to discovering the message of the stories and to delivering that message in an accurate, relevant, clear, and inspiring manner. He shows the reader how to select a complete unit of thought, identify its theological and historical contexts, discern its plot, determine its original theological message, and craft its take-home truth. From there he shows how to construct a sermon that will not only inform listeners, but convince them to 'buy' and live out the take-home truth of the passage. As I read through the book, I found myself thinking: *Yes, that makes sense! What a good idea! Why haven't I been doing this?* This will really enhance my preaching!"

**Robert B. Chisholm, Jr.,
Chair and Senior Professor of Old Testament Studies,
Dallas Theological Seminary**

"In *Preaching Old Testament Narratives*, Ben Walton provides a clear, helpful, and thoughtful approach to preaching from this important genre. The book is well designed, enabling the experienced or novice preacher a clear path toward biblical preaching."

**Scott M. Gibson,
Haddon W. Robinson Professor of Preaching and Ministry,
Gordon-Conwell Theological Seminary**

"The biblical text—specifically, the theology of the text—is what preachers are called to proclaim. Nailing down the theological message of Old Testament narratives is notoriously difficult. Walton has written an excellent how-to guide for preachers. Like the sermons he espouses, Walton's book is accurate, relevant, clear, and inspiring. It will instruct rookie preachers, challenge veteran preachers, and inspire all preachers to work hard at their craft. Practical and profound, Walton's book is a worthy addition to every preacher's library."

**Brandon Cash, Director, Preaching and Pastoral Ministry Program,
Talbot School of Theology, Biola University**

"Everyone loves a story. The power of the narrative has not disappeared. We are still captivated by a good story well told. And the Old Testament is a treasure trove of stories. Yet, the Old Testament narrative presents exegetical and homiletical challenges that any serious student of the Word will have to wrestle with. And the tension often lies between being faithful to the ancient text and making the sermon relevant. There are preachers who focus on the meaning of the biblical text, but sometimes at the expense of making the text meaningful to listeners. How can we remain faithful to the preaching of the Word without failing to engage our listeners today?

"To answer this dilemma, Dr. Ben Walton proposes that we consider three aspects of communication—words, genre, and message—as possible ways forward. Pastors, seminary students, and all who communicate God's Word should consider Dr. Walton's suggestions on how to preach with biblical integrity and homiletical clarity."

**Desmond Soh, Assistant Professor of Homiletics
and Intercultural Studies, Singapore Bible College**

"Walton's careful analysis of a specific narrative is a helpful model that exemplifies the interpretation of narrative texts for preaching. His writing is lucid and dynamic, and his presence is felt at your side, a friendly guide helping you along as you make your way through the narrative of 2 Samuel 11–12. In his writing he has modeled the 'four pillars of excellent preaching' that he propounds: accuracy, clarity, relevance, and inspiring quality."

**Abraham Kuruvilla, Research Professor of Pastoral Ministries,
Dallas Theological Seminary**

PREACHING
Old Testament
NARRATIVES

BENJAMIN H. WALTON

Preaching Old Testament Narratives
© 2016 by Benjamin H. Walton

Published by Kregel Publications, a division of Kregel, Inc., 2450 Oak Industrial Dr. NE, Grand Rapids, MI 49505-6020.

All rights reserved. No part of this book may be reproduced, stored in a retrieval system, or transmitted in any form or by any means—electronic, mechanical, photocopy, recording, or otherwise—without written permission of the publisher, except for brief quotations in printed reviews.

All Scripture quotations, unless otherwise indicated, are from The Holy Bible, English Standard Version® (ESV®), copyright © 2001 by Crossway, a publishing ministry of Good News Publishers. Used by permission. All rights reserved.

ISBN 978-0-8254-4258-2

Printed in the United States of America
16 17 18 19 20 / 5 4 3 2 1

Donald Sunukjian and Jeffrey Arthurs

Molders of preachers, least of all me

Contents

Foreword 17
Preface 19
Introduction 21
Abbreviations 25

Part I: Discover the Message

1. OT Narratives, Hermeneutics, and Biblical Authority 29
What Does It Mean to Preach with Biblical Authority? 29
Hermeneutics 101: How Words and Genre Work Together to
   Communicate Messages 31
Hermeneutics 201: Comparing OT Narratives and NT Epistles 33
   Objection One: Apostolic and Early Church Hermeneutics 36
   Objection Two: 1 Corinthians 10:1–22 37
Original-Theological Message and Take-Home Truth 39
   The Benefits of OTMs and THTs 41
   Mistakes in the Application of OT Narratives 42
      Springboarding 42
      Biblical Model Approach 42
      Illustrated Principles Approach 42
      Universalizing the Plot Line Approach 43

2. OT Narratives: From Text Selection to Take-Home Truth 45
Overview of the Steps 46
Step 1: Select a Complete Unit of Thought 47
   Complete Plot 48
   Beginning and End Markers 49
Step 2: Identify the Theological and Historical Contexts 50
   Theological Context 50

Historical Context 52
    Ancient Israel's View of the Retribution Principle and
        Afterlife 52
    Latest Old Covenant Expansion 53
    Original Audience 54
Step 3: Study the Plot 56
    Write Scene Summaries 57
    Identify Main Characters 58
    Find Out What the Narrative Dwells On 60
    Ask Good Questions and Get Good Answers 61
    Select Quality Reference Works 65
Step 4: Determine the Original-Theological Message 66
    Theological Analysis of Structural Commentary 68
        Previous CUTs 68
        Comments by the Narrator 69
        Repeated Words or Phrases 70
    Theological Analysis of Characters 70
    Theological Analysis of Each Scene 71
        Analyze the Dialogue 72
        Analyze the Action 75
    Write the Original-Theological Message 77
        Guideline 1: Be Accurate 77
        Guideline 2: Be Precise 78
        Guideline 3: Write One Complete, Crisp, and Immediately
            Understandable Sentence 78
        Guideline 4: Avoid "and" 79
        Guideline 5: Simultaneously Determine the Question the
            OTM Answers 79
Step 5: Craft the Take-Home Truth 81

3. A Succinct Commentary on 2 Samuel 11–12 83
Introduction to 2 Samuel 10–20 83
Latest Old Covenant Expansion 84
From Text Selection to Take-Home Truth for 2 Samuel 11–12 85
    Step 1: Select a Complete Unit of Thought 85

Step 2: Identify the Theological and Historical Contexts 85
Step 3: Study the Plot 86
Step 4: Determine the Original-Theological Message 86
Step 5: Craft the Take-Home Truth 87

Part II: Deliver the Message

4. Initial Considerations **91**
Four Pillars of Excellent Preaching 91
   Accuracy 91
   Relevance 92
   Clarity 93
   Inspiring 94
Common Approaches to Preaching OT Narratives 97
   Verse-by-Verse 97
   Alliteration 98
   Principlization 98
   Big Idea 99
   Mini-Synopses 100

5. Create the Introduction **103**
Major Aims of an Introduction 103
   Identification 103
      Is the Preacher Like Me? 105
      Does the Preacher Like Me? 106
      Does the Preacher Meet My Expectations? 110
   Establish Relevance 110
   Prepare Listeners to Follow the Rest of the Sermon 111
Stages of an Introduction 112
   Engage and Focus 112
      Brief Story or Illustration 114
      First Half of a Picture-Painting Application 115
      Explore an Intriguing Issue 117
      Refer to a Recent Event 120
      Involve the Listeners 121

  How Not to Open a Sermon 123
  Set the Stage 124
  Preview and Announce the Passage 126

6. Preach through the CUT (Part 1): Movements **129**
 Selecting Verses for Movements 130
 Crafting Excellent Movements 131
  Guideline 1: Don't Word Movements Like Main Points 131
  Guideline 2: Keep the Sermon Squarely on the Focus/THT .. 132
  Guideline 3: Put the Fruit of Sermon Preparation into Them ... 132
  Guideline 4: Make Connections to Real Life 134
  Guideline 5: Write/Speak for the Ear 134
   Tips #1 and 2: Use Spoken Grammar and Short Sentences 135
   Tip #3: Incorporate Dialogue 135
   Tip #4: Cut Down on the Pronouns 136
   Tip #5: Speak of Past Events as if They Are Happening Now .. 137

7. Preach through the CUT (Part 2): Other Options **139**
 Summarize-without-Reading 139
 Explain-as-You-Read 141
  First Verse of the CUT 142
  To Accentuate the Text's Drama 142
 Lead-In 143

8. State the Take-Home Truth **147**
 As We Preach through the Text 148
 After We Preach through the Text 152

9. Help Listeners "Buy" the Take-Home Truth **155**
 Two Components of Overcoming Objections 156
  Raise the Objection 156
  Overcome the Objection 157
 Reasons People Don't Buy THTs from OT Narratives 158
  They Can't Systematize It 158
  They Value Something Else Even More 159

10. Develop Picture-Painting Applications ... 163
Initial Objections to PPAs ... 165
Keys to Effectiveness ... 166
    Relax ... 166
    Tie It to the Take-Home Truth ... 166
    Identify Applicable Situations ... 166
    Be Realistic ... 168
    Show More Than Tell ... 168
Template ... 169
    Transition ... 169
    Setting ... 169
    Problem ... 170
    Rationalization ... 170
    Plot Twist ... 171
    Biblical Response ... 171
    Possible Outcome(s) and Long-Term Benefit ... 172
    Variations ... 173
        Half & Half ... 173
        Pre-Existing Situations ... 173
        Compact ... 175

11. Move to Christ ... 177
What Does the Bible Mean by "Preaching Christ"? ... 178
    Preaching Christ in the Gospels ... 179
        The Use of the OT in the Gospels ... 179
        Extent to Which Christ Is Found in the OT ... 180
        Jesus on the Influence of the New Covenant for Preaching from the OT ... 182
    Preaching Christ in Acts ... 183
    Preaching Christ in 1–2 Corinthians ... 184
    Preaching Christ in Colossians ... 184
    Conclusions ... 185
How Can We Seamlessly Move to Christ? ... 185
    Two Criteria for Seamlessly Moving to Christ ... 186
    Informal Moves to Christ ... 187

    Formal (Pre-Conclusion) Move to Christ 188
        Ask How/Why Christ Makes the THT Possible 188
        Show How the Text Reminds Us of the Need for Christ 189
        Christiconic 189
        Greidanus' Seven Ways 190

12. Finishing Well in the Conclusion 193
    Elements of a Conclusion 193
        Review 194
        Final Push 194
        Closing Affirmation 195
    Mistakes to Avoid 196

13. From Good to Excellent 199
    Pray 199
    Dedicate Fifteen Focused Hours to Sermon Preparation 200
    Use Humor 201
    Add a Little Creativity 203
        Enhance the Multi-Sensory Appeal 204
        Preach a First Person Narrative Sermon Occasionally 205
    Deliver the Message Smoothly 205
    Maintain a Disciplined Tongue 206
        Be Real 207
        Be Winsome 208
        Be Careful with Self-Disclosure 209
    Write a Manuscript, Then Ditch It 211
    Practice the Sermon 212
    Get a Preaching Coach 213

    Appendix A: Organic Sermon Structure 215
    Appendix B: Sermon from 2 Samuel 11–12 217
    Appendix C: Sermon from Genesis 11:1–9 231
    Appendix D: Storyline of the Old Testament 241
    Bibliography 249
    About the Author 255

Foreword
Jeffrey Arthurs

Haddon Robinson was fond of saying that for the pastor, "Sundays roll around with amazing regularity—every three or four days!" Similarly, I heard Timothy Keller say in a panel discussion that the task of preparing sermons is "relentless." What preachers need is a doable method for preparing sermons that is both exegetically sound and rhetorically savvy. That's what Benjamin Walton has provided. This book is a template, well-illustrated, for how to manage the relentless task of feeding your flock from the pulpit.

Part of the reason the task is daunting is because preachers stand between two worlds; we exegete both the text and the audience. In the case of Benjamin Walton's focus, that text will be an Old Testament narrative, and it's no easy task to uncover the theology of a story. That is because stories "show" more than they "tell." Biblical narrators are theologians, yes, but they are also artists who use deft brushstrokes to depict the excellences of God, the folly of humans, the glory of redemption, and the sobering warning of judgment. So I say again that preachers need a do-able, realistic method for discovering the theologian-artist's intention. We are interpreters of Scripture.

And preachers are also persuaders. This moves us into the realm of rhetoric as we contextualize the ancient narratives for the twenty-first century mission field. As communicators we apply the truth, speak for the ear, address objections, and deliver in a way that embodies the message rather than contradicting it. Is such a method available? Read on.

Preachers do one more thing as well. They not only interpret and communicate Scripture. They also watch souls. Preaching cannot be divorced from shepherding. Perhaps it is more accurate to say that soul-watching is not a third component of pulpit ministry; rather that it is the sum total of that ministry. Our roles as interpreters and communicators serve this overarching role. You will see that emphasis in Dr. Walton's book. It is a gift to busy pastors who stand between two worlds every three or four days.

Preface

When I put together a few notes about OT narratives fifteen years ago for a class at church, I could never have imagined it would become the book you hold in your hands today. It was hard enough back then to imagine writing a ten-page paper! A book it has become, and hopefully it's one that will serve you well.

My goal was to create a resource that you'll want to turn to when you preach OT narratives. My heart is for practitioners—those who stand before God's Word and God's people, and who are called to be faithful to both. Multiple times over the last few years, as the book developed, its contents were read and tested anonymously by groups of pastors. Their feedback encouraged and challenged me to meet them where they (and you) are at.

The book is unique in that it fleshes out in one volume both the interpretive and practical skills necessary to preach OT narratives with excellence. These skills have proven to be learnable among a cross-section of pastors. I pray they enrich your study of Scripture, deepen your faith in God, and enhance your service to others. We preachers desire to preach God's Word faithfully and powerfully. It's my hope that after closely following the book's approach, you'll have an intuitive sense that you have done just that.

Chapters 4–10 are a conscious attempt to apply, in my own way, Donald Sunukjian's homiletic to the preaching of OT narratives. Don is a homiletical genius and the author of *Invitation to Biblical Preaching*. A seminary provost once told me that experienced pastors appreciate Don's teaching so much that he consistently receives the highest marks from them when he comes to town to teach doctoral-level courses.

Many thanks are in order. Thanks first to my wife, Sara, and my boys Colin, Lucas, and Landon. I delight in you. Thanks also to longtime friends Jim Sides, Scott Elliott, and Tom Wise. Who would have known?

I would like to offer special thanks to Dennis Hillman, Shawn Vander Lugt, Laura Bartlett, and the rest of the team at Kregel. Thanks for seeing value in the book and for shepherding it along the path to publication.

I remain in awe of God for blessing me with an eclectic mix of professors who were ideally suited to develop this future homiletician: Jerry Camery-Hoggatt, Ben Shin, Peter Anders, Alan Hultberg, Tim Ralston, Randy Pelton, Jeff Arthurs, and Don Sunukjian.

The book is dedicated to Don Sunukjian of Talbot School of Theology, Biola University, and to Jeff Arthurs of Gordon-Conwell Theological Seminary. A finer combination of homileticians who can find? Don taught me to preach and allowed me to lecture and mentor his students. Jeff was my doctoral mentor. His investment of time enabled me to polish my preaching skills in ways that only regular feedback from an experienced pro could.

Introduction

Three pastors. Different backgrounds. The same struggle.

Pastor John
John has led First Church for five years. A graduate of National Seminary, he maintains some facility in the biblical languages. When he preaches, he makes use of interlinears, lexicons, and the best commentaries. He's most comfortable in the NT letters, but occasionally preaches OT narratives.

He's currently preaching through 2 Samuel. He's begun, however, to question how well he's doing. "Am I going too fast or too slow?" His goal is to preach one complete unit of thought (CUT) at a time, but he has difficulty figuring out where they begin and end. The commentaries are of little help because they break up passages in all sorts of ways, and use terms like "literary unit" to describe everything from blocks of dialogue to ten or more chapters.

He's also questioning his application. He understands that it isn't something preachers make up. It derives from the message of the text. He tends to use the old "When you are in a situation similar to the one in the biblical story, God will respond to you pretty much the same way he responded to them" approach, but he's beginning to doubt its validity.

John's got the details down. What he needs is a resource that helps him put the pieces together, so that he can maximize his preaching potential from OT narratives.

Pastor Shawn
Shawn has led Second Church for ten years. A former student of Regional Seminary, he spent a decade in ministry before becoming a senior pastor. He gave up trying to use scholarly commentaries years ago: "It's difficult to get much out of them. They're full of minutiae, addressing concerns few of us care about." What he finds most useful are the commentaries of Big Preacher.

Shawn would differ with anyone who questions the quality of his preaching—so would his congregation. He's no topical preacher. "We preach verse-by-verse here." He's currently preaching through 2 Samuel, one chapter per week. He rarely questions the accuracy of his applications, and while he doesn't think of it this way, he "applies" the Bible by reading a few verses, sharing what comes to mind, reading a few more verses, and sharing more personal reflections.

Shawn wants to preach OT narratives with biblical authority, but needs a resource that helps him bridge the gap between scholarly commentaries and the sermon, so that he can maximize his preaching potential from OT narratives.

Pastor Ron
Ron has led Third Church for fifteen years. He never went to seminary but has taken a few Bible classes. Currently, he's too busy with a thriving ministry to pursue a seminary education. Besides, what if seminary killed his ministry? It killed the ministry of Associate Pastor's son. "He gave up a great future here because seminary made him think that my preaching and evangelism are unbiblical."

Ron usually covers a variety of passages in his sermons. With OT narratives, however, he finds it better to stick with one passage. He sees important lessons in them: how to have hope and courage; how to be great husbands and wives; and how to pray, listen to God's voice, and discern his will. This week, he'll preach on how to avoid marital infidelity from 2 Samuel 11. He sees the value of commentaries for lecture preachers, and never questions the accuracy of his applications because he finds that most passages are pretty clear. When he needs it, he finds Favorite Author to be helpful.

Ron values accuracy in preaching, but needs a resource—one that minimizes academic lingo, so that he can maximize his preaching potential from OT narratives.

Despite their differences, John, Shawn, and Ron have the same struggle: to preach OT narratives with excellence. This book is designed to help preachers like them.

Abbreviations

OT   Old Testament
NT   New Testament

CUT   Complete Unit of Thought
EI   Exegetical Idea
OTM   Original-Theological Message
PPA   Picture-Painting Application
THT   Take-Home Truth

v(v).   Verse(s) in the chapter under discussion

ISBE   International Standard Bible Encyclopedia

Part I:
Discover the Message

CHAPTER 1

OT NARRATIVES, HERMENEUTICS, AND BIBLICAL AUTHORITY

Accuracy in preaching is vital in today's world. In the 800s, it mattered less if preachers thought the Bible taught the earth was the center of the universe. Everyone believed that. In the 1400s, it mattered less if preachers taught a flat earth. People believed the clergy more than university professors.

Today, when we misinterpret Scripture or assert knowledge of God or his will that the Bible doesn't teach, repercussions can be serious. A few years ago, I had a chance at a college graduation party to witness to a young man who had left the faith years earlier. He was a strip-club bouncer. Knowing that I was a pastor, he asked me a number of Bible questions. My answers shocked him because I was able to show him that the Bible didn't teach much of the well-intentioned legalism he grew up with. No fancy interpretations were necessary. No in-depth analysis was needed—only the most well-accepted, but neglected, principles of biblical interpretation.

What Does It Mean to Preach with Biblical Authority?

Preaching with biblical authority means that our sermons accurately proclaim and apply the message of their biblical preaching texts. It has little to do with whether the sermon is verse-by-verse, topical, or otherwise. It's often called "expository preaching" or "biblical preaching." The benefit of preaching with biblical authority is significant: It renders our message God's message.

Preaching with biblical authority is rooted in the historic Christian belief that God is so different than us that the only reliable way to have knowledge of God or his will is through Scripture. Applied to the sermon, it's the idea that unless the messages we preach and the applications we give derive from the message of our preaching texts, there is a good chance we've misrepresented God.

Preaching with biblical authority has one fundamental problem: It requires preachers. That's you and me. Keith Mathison once observed that no one "asserts that a Bible can enter a pulpit and preach itself. No one asserts that a Bible can read itself. Scripture cannot be interpreted or preached apart from the involvement of some human agency."[1] Since preaching with biblical authority is an action more than a belief, it requires more than a theoretical commitment. It must be put into practice. Despite his profound admiration for us preachers, Haddon Robinson admits that preaching with biblical authority "has suffered severely in the pulpits of those claiming to be its friends."[2]

To preach with biblical authority, we must use sound hermeneutics. *Hermeneutics is the thoughtful process of discovering what a biblical text was designed to teach those it was originally written to, so that we can faithfully apply it to our lives today.* It recognizes that careful thought is necessary to interpret and apply the Bible. Hermeneutics is necessary to overcome the temptation to too hastily equate our thoughts with God's thoughts. When we preach without giving much thought to hermeneutics, we relegate the Bible to the status of a tool—a tool for us preachers to carry out our agendas, which always seems noble to us.

---

1. Mathison, *The Shape of Sola Scriptura*, 259.
2. Robinson, *Biblical Preaching*, 4.

Hermeneutics 101:
How Words and Genre Work Together
to Communicate Messages

Sound hermeneutics requires an understanding of how communication works. The Bible, after all, is God's authoritative communication to us. We need to consider three aspects of communication: words, genre, and message. "Words" refers to what we say; "genre" to the way we say it; and "message" to the reason for saying it.[3] When we decide to communicate, we first determine the point we want to make (message); then the way we want to say it (genre); and then finally, we express ourselves in words.

Of these three, genre is the most neglected by preachers. Genre is an essential clue to understanding the message of biblical texts because it clues us in to the reading strategy—i.e., the hermeneutical principles—that the biblical author expects us to use. We practice genre analysis every day. We've all mastered the reading strategies of dozens of genres, including tax bills, political cartoons, parodies, fairy tales, editorials, and street signs. We don't think we're engaging in genre analysis because these genres are common in our culture.

Words alone cannot communicate a message. Genre is necessary to make sense of words. Take the phrase "I am bad." We're familiar with the wording, but what is the message? If intended ironically, it is, "I think I'm cool." If it's a mocking insult, the message is, "The person I'm speaking about thinks he's cool, but he's not." If it's a heartfelt confession, the message is, "I believe that I am a bad person."

In some genres, the words are similar to the message. In others, they are quite different. Let's say we want others to believe that our kids are great. If we want to be crystal clear but dry, we could use a declarative sentence. If we want to "wow" our listeners, we could use an anecdote. If we want to rouse the emotions, we could write a poem. Notice that even when the message is the same, the genre we couch it in affects our word choice:

---

3. Klein, Blomberg, and Hubbard, *Introduction to Biblical Interpretation*, 9, 169.

Genre: Declarative sentence
Words: My kids are great.
Message: Believe my kids are great.

Genre: Anecdote
Words: I woke up, got coffee, heard laughs outside, and saw my kids washing my car.
Message: Believe my kids are great.

Genre: Poem
Words: Roses are red, violets are blue, my kids' hearts are true.
Message: Believe my kids are great.

The same dynamics are present in biblical communication. In some genres, the words are similar to the message; in others, they are very different.

Genre: Direct command (Eph. 5:18a)
Words: Do not get drunk on wine, which is debauchery.
Message: Do not get drunk on alcoholic beverages, which is a public act of wild living.

Genre: Parable (Matt. 13:44)
Words: The kingdom of heaven is like treasure hidden in a field. When found, the finder hides it, sells everything, and buys the field.
Message: Join the kingdom of heaven; it's more valuable than anything else.

Genre: Lament (Ps. 10)
Words: God, why do you hide? The wicked are prospering. God, fix the problem. God is great.
Message: When feeling like God is hiding in the midst of an unjust trial, God's people *can* (express their

feelings to God) call on God to fix the problem; and, when they do, do it while maintaining full confidence that God is great.

Genre: OT narrative (Gen. 11:1–9)
Words: After the flood, people don't disperse, endangering and defying God's redemptive plans, so God disperses them.
Message: It is futile to defy God's redemptive plans, because God's redemptive plans will prevail.

To give an example from recent history: A few years ago, *The Da Vinci Code* caused quite a stir because many read it more like a work of history than like the novel it is. This was largely a result of the author employing a literary device in its opening pages to heighten interest in the story. The gullible public, unfamiliar with fiction's tools of the trade and unversed in historical Jesus studies, misread the book in droves and made its author a very rich man. If misreading genre clues in secular literature can have deleterious effects, how much more when biblical literature is preached?

Hermeneutics 201: Comparing OT Narratives and NT Epistles

We call the message of a biblical text its theology. This is because the message is from God, and it makes demands on our lives. It includes both the primary and ancillary theological principles that God inspired a text to communicate. A text's message/theology represents the future-oriented direction of the text. In other words, its goal is to get us to conform our lives to it going forward.

Old Testament narratives differ from NT epistles in three key ways. The first is that OT narratives are a form of indirect communication. New Testament epistles are a form of direct communication. The messages of NT epistolary texts are clearer, more straightforward. They often use reason and logic to make their points. Old Testament narratives, however, seek to persuade by enrapturing us in their stories, thereby causing us to lower our defenses, so that their messages can land easily and affectively on our hearts.

The second key difference between OT narratives and NT epistles is that the complete units of thought (CUTs) of OT narratives tend to be one to two chapters in length. The size of NT epistolary CUTs tend to be one to two paragraphs. Identifying CUTs is crucial because they provide the smallest unit of textual context that *must* be considered when interpreting anything within their boundaries.

The third key difference is that *unlike NT epistles, OT narratives do a lot of describing and not a lot of prescribing.* That is, they say a lot about what happened and only a little about what should have happened or must happen in the future. Compare 2 Samuel 11:1 with Colossians 2:6–7:

2 Samuel 11:1 (OT Narrative)	Colossians 2:6–7 (NT Epistle)
In the spring of the year, the time when kings go out to battle, David sent Joab, and his servants with him, and all Israel. And they ravaged the Ammonites and besieged Rabbah. But David remained at Jerusalem.	Therefore, as you received Christ Jesus the Lord, so walk in him, rooted and built up in him and established in the faith, just as you were taught, abounding in thanksgiving.

It's at this point that an important hermeneutical principle comes into play: *"Unless Scripture explicitly tells us we must do something, what is only narrated or described does not function in a normative (i.e., obligatory) way—unless it can be demonstrated on other grounds that the author intended it to function in this way."*[4] In other words, it

---

4. Fee and Stuart, *How to Read the Bible for All Its Worth*, 124. See also Klein, Blomberg, and Hubbard, *Introduction to Biblical Interpretation*, 424.

is illegitimate—going beyond the bounds of biblical authority—to turn the individual actions or behaviors that a text describes into principles or commands to be obeyed, unless we can make a really good case for it. Ignoring this hermeneutical principle is called *atomistic* interpretation

You might be wondering, "How can I know when a described behavior is prescribed?" The answer is: through a careful examination of a combination of factors (1) in a CUT or (2) its book that work together to prescribe the behavior being described. For example, in terms of factors in a CUT, most of 2 Samuel 11 describes David's murderous activities. At the end of the chapter we read, "But the thing that David had done displeased the LORD" (11:27). From this combination of factors, it is accurate to conclude that "murder is wrong, even for the king."[5]

When we take these three key differences between OT narratives and NT epistles together, an important point emerges: *OT narratives convey a small number of theological principles.* The number of theological principles in one or two chapters of OT narrative pale in comparison to one or two chapters of NT epistle. Plus, as we just saw in the 2 Samuel 11–12 example, it usually takes at least half of a narrative CUT for even ancillary theological principles to be taught.

For preaching, this means that OT narratives contain very few legitimate application principles. What is application? *Application is an actionable principle, instruction, or exemplification that derives from the theology (message) of a biblical text.* Application is not a universally true or even biblically true idea that comes to our minds when we read or preach a text. Application is not a principle that we "see" illustrated in a text. It is a requirement of God that is prescribed by the passage at hand, or a way to carry out such a requirement. Gordon Fee and Douglas Stuart express it well:

---

5. For discovering how (and how difficult it is) to discern exceptions through a combination of factors in a biblical book, see Wenham, *Story as Torah: Reading Old Testament Narrative Ethically.*

Perhaps the single most useful bit of caution we can give you about reading and learning from narratives is this: Do not be a monkey-see-monkey-do reader [or preacher] of the Bible. . . . An Old Testament narrative usually *illustrates* a doctrine [or behavior] *taught* propositionally *elsewhere*. . . . Narratives record what happened—not necessarily what should have happened. . . . Therefore, not every narrative has an individual identifiable moral application [i.e., a specific behavior that it is advocating or warning against]. . . . We are not always told at the end of a narrative whether what happened was good or bad. We are expected to be able to [not apply, but] judge this on the basis of what God has *taught* us directly and categorically *elsewhere* in Scripture.[6]

Objection One: Apostolic and Early Church Hermeneutics

I commonly hear two objections when I share that the theology of an OT narrative contains only a small number of application principles. The first cites the hermeneutics of the apostles or early church, suggesting that they had an alternative method of applying OT narratives that we can use today.

Two things can be said in reply. The first, which relates to apostolic hermeneutics, is that if you are willing to dedicate three to five years of your life to sort out and learn the actual hermeneutical methods of the apostles—as opposed to some hack pseudo-version of it—go for it. Don't be surprised, however, when you discover that much of what they did pertained not to discerning life application principles from every nook and cranny of an OT narrative, but to pointing to Christ from the OT.

The second, which relates to the early church's hermeneutics, is that while the early church didn't always recover the message of an OT narrative, it doesn't mean that it wasn't their goal to do so. That many tried and failed doesn't mean that we should fail intentionally. Further, in many ways correct hermeneutics involves what

---

6. Fee and Stuart, *How to Read the Bible for All Its Worth*, 110–11 (emphasis added).

the early church called the "four senses" of Scripture. This way of thinking about the hermeneutical process was dropped not because it was altogether invalid, but because its consistent misapplication yielded highly improbable results.

Objection Two: 1 Corinthians 10:1–22

The second objection that I commonly hear is, "Doesn't the apostle Paul teach in 1 Corinthians 10:1–22, especially 10:6, that we can moralize—i.e., *atomistically* turn the individual actions of OT narrative characters into 'do or do not do as the biblical character did' principles or commands?" The answer is "no."

There are three ways we can know this. The first way is by carefully reading 1 Corinthians 10:6. Paul—who, in the surrounding context of 10:1–11:1, is warning the Corinthians to avoid idolatry—refers to certain OT narratives that teach the futility of idolatry (i.e., trusting in anything other than God for a sense of national, family, personal, or economic security). As part of that argument, he says in 1 Corinthians 10:6:

> **"Now these things took place as** examples
>
> > [*tupos*: "*model, pattern*. . . . —b. as guidance for a style of life. . . . 1 Cor 10:6. . . . —c. of someth. serving as a model for understanding someth. else, usually rendered 'type'. . . . 1 Cor 10:6][7]
>
> **for us, [so] that we might not desire evil [e.g., idolatry] as they did."**

In other words, 1 Corinthians 10:6 teaches that certain OT narratives record Israel's idolatry, so that future generations of people

---

7. Danker, *The Concise Greek-English Lexicon of the New Testament*, 358. This is a quasi-abridgement and lexical enhancement of Bauer, Danker, et al., *A Greek-English Lexicon of the New Testament and Other Early Christian Literature*.

would not follow the overall "model" or "pattern" of idolatry in those narratives. They were written so that we would not be a "type" or "contemporary version" of people who in some sense align ourselves with God, but are in fact idolaters. What Paul is *not* saying is that OT narratives were written so that we would *atomistically* make application out of the individual actions of a character.

So then, while it would be legitimate to say, at some point in the sermon, something general like, "Let's be faithful (or not stumble) like Israel in this passage," it would be illegitimate to *atomistically* turn the specific actions of OT narrative characters into principles or commands to emulate or avoid.

The second way that we can know 1 Corinthians 10:1–22 doesn't teach us to moralize is by looking at the applications that Paul makes. They are: Do not participate in idolatry, particularly of a sexual variety (vv. 7–8); do not put God/Christ to the test (v. 9); do not grumble against God's authority as expressed through the words of his divinely appointed Old Covenant prophets and New Covenant apostles (v. 10); humble yourselves before God (v. 12); believe that God is faithful, enabling victory over temptation (v. 13); flee idolatry (v. 14); people cannot genuinely worship God while still participating in idolatrous practices (v. 21); it is a bad idea to arouse God's jealousy through participation in idolatrous practices because God is stronger than us (v. 22).[8] As we'll see, Paul is not moralizing because he is not atomistically making application out of an action.

For example, Paul's application in 1 Corinthians 10:10 is, "Do not grumble against God's authority." This application derives from either Numbers 14 or 16, it's unclear which. Nonetheless, in both of these chapters, does Israel grumble against God's authority? Yes. Is the application in 1 Corinthians 10:10 that we should not do that same action? Yes. Did Paul moralize? No.

Here's why: As we discussed earlier and illustrated with an example from 2 Samuel 11–12, OT narratives occasionally teach that

---

8. Fee, *The First Epistle to the Corinthians*, 486–524.

an action by a character is good or bad. This occurs when a combination of factors in a CUT or its book work together to make that point. In Numbers 14, vv. 19–20 comment on Israel's grumbling in vv. 1–3 and indicate that it was sinful. In Numbers 16, vv. 42–47 contain God's immediate reaction to Israel's grumbling in v. 41, indicating that it too was sinful. Thus Paul's application is legitimate, because a combination of factors working together in the CUT makes that point.

Third, we can know that Paul's applications in 1 Corinthians 10:1–22 are not the result of moralizing because they apply the primary—"trust God alone"— theological principle of their CUTs. The next chapter discusses how to discern that. Before we move on, however, let's reflect on the words of Peter Vogt:

> Understanding the author's purposes in writing a narrative helps us avoid a common error in the interpretation of narratives. Many times we approach narratives and look for a readily applicable "moral" that is relevant to our lives. But sound interpretation of the text means seeking to understand the author's intention, not simply looking for something readily applicable.[S]ound interpretation means being content with (or, at least, accepting) the [text on its terms].[9]

Original-Theological Message and Take-Home Truth

In our discussion so far, we've defined the "message" of a biblical text and equated it with its "theology." We've discussed how the message/theology of a passage often contains primary and ancillary theological principles, although OT narratives contain few ancillary theological principles. At this point, I want to introduce and define two terms, Original-Theological Message (OTM) and Take-Home Truth (THT):

---

9. Vogt, *Interpreting the Pentateuch*, 51.

OTM: The primary theological principle that a biblical text was designed to communicate to its original audience.

THT: A timeless or contemporary expression of the OTM.[10]

The THT is the message of the sermon. It takes the time-specific language of the OTM and replaces it with timeless or contemporary equivalents.[11] Therefore, we have to determine the OTM before we determine the THT. As we'll discuss in chapter 2, moving from the time-specific language of the OTM to the timeless or contemporary language of the THT requires the building of legitimate hermeneutical bridges. For 2 Samuel 11–12, the OTM and THT are:

OTM: <u>The Lord</u> will use <u>repentant kings of Israel</u> to fulfill <u>the Davidic Covenant</u>, but <u>despising the Lord's word</u> brings discipline.

THT: <u>God</u> will use <u>us</u> to fulfill <u>his plan of salvation</u>, but <u>sin</u> brings discipline.

Since OT narratives teach few theological principles and usually only one unifies a passage, the THT is generally going to be the only principle we will spend time applying. That said, when we cover 2 Samuel 11:27 in a sermon from 2 Samuel 11–12, we may want to say something like, "You see, murder is wrong. For you. Me. And the king." To spend much more time on it, however, would disrupt the coherence, clarity, and flow of the sermon.

Since an entire CUT is necessary to communicate a THT, we will generally need to wait until after the narrative has been covered before making application. *Nevertheless, the entire sermon should be relevant in the sense that we should relate the text to real life throughout*

---

10. The term comes from Sunukjian, *Invitation to Biblical Preaching*, 65–84.
11. Some modifications to this method would be necessary for preaching from the OT Law, but that's a discussion for another book!

the sermon. For example, when covering 2 Samuel 11:1–2, we might say something like:

> The story opens with two pictures: One of David, the other of Israel's army. Like a vacationing CEO who demands his employees double-down on their hours, we find David taking a siesta, his entire army out in battle. Read with me verses 1–2.

Nevertheless, we would go beyond the bounds of biblical authority to *atomistically* apply this detail by saying something like, "When we're lazy, we risk falling into sin." While we may "see" this principle illustrated, the passage doesn't teach it. Furthermore, like so many principles we "see" illustrated in the Bible, careful study reveals the need for corrective lenses. In this case, David's decision to stay home, like the CEO's to vacation, wasn't sinful.[12]

The Benefits of OTMs and THTs

There are two powerful benefits of OTMs and THTs. First, they anchor the sermon to the primary message God wanted to get across with that biblical text. It stands to reason that the primary message God inspired a passage to teach should generally be our primary message. We could call OTMs and THTs our "authority maximizers."

Second, OTMs and THTs promote sermon coherence and unity by enabling us to check everything we want to say by them. Unless there is a really good reason, if something we want to say does not help our listeners understand, buy, or apply the THT, it should be taken out of the sermon. Thus, we could also call OTMs and THTs our "effectiveness maximizers."

I've had some protest: "I'm not into that 'big idea' stuff." Fair enough, but as kids are told, "You can choose your behavior, but you can't control the consequences." We can choose to ignore the proven principles of oral clarity—and if we have a charismatic

---

12. Firth, *1 & 2 Samuel*, 417.

sense about us, attendance numbers may increase—but listeners are not going to be able to follow or internalize our sermons, not even with bulletin notes!

Mistakes in the Application of OT Narratives

Since knowing what *not* to do can clarify what to do, this section discusses a few common ways that preachers *mis*apply OT narratives. To avoid redundancy, I will discuss them without rehashing previously discussed arguments against them.

Springboarding

Springboarding occurs when we use the biblical text as "a peg on which to hang a string of [our own] ideas."[13] It's a venerable method that's been around for years. Back in the 1940s, Paul Warren noted that too often preachers "use" the biblical text "simply as a rallying point for [their] own ideas."[14] Many springboarders are heralded as biblical preachers because their frequent—even verse-by-verse—references to the biblical text give the impression that they're faithfully proclaiming and applying the text.

Biblical Model Approach

The Biblical Model Approach is a form of moralizing that turns OT narratives into "how-to" lists of principles, which they inevitably don't teach. This method might turn the story of Gideon and his fleece in Judges 6:36–40 into a misleading sermon on how to discern God's will. Likewise, it might turn the story of David and Goliath in 1 Samuel 17 into a message—that the Bible nowhere teaches—on overcoming adversity "God's way."

Illustrated Principles Approach

The Illustrated Principles Approach is a form of moralizing that "applies" the principles that preachers "see" illustrated in a biblical

---

13. Stibbs, *Expounding God's Word*, 67.
14. Warren, "By What Authority? Pitfalls in Pulpit Interpretation," 208.

narrative. This approach might turn David's decision to stay home from battle in 2 Samuel 11:1 into an anti-laziness principle. Likewise, it might turn David's decision to look at Bathsheba bathing in 2 Samuel 11:2–5 into a warning about the need to flee temptation.

Universalizing the Plot Line Approach

In seminary, students are taught the skill of creating exegetical (big) ideas: long, complex sentences that summarize the details of their texts. It's a worthwhile skill to learn. There is a qualitative difference, however, between the exegetical ideas of most NT epistolary texts and OT narratives. For example, the exegetical ideas of most NT epistolary texts are prescriptive statements of their theology. The exegetical ideas of OT narratives, however, are *descriptive* statements of their plot line.

Without taking this difference into account, the Universalizing the Plot Line Approach confuses an OT narrative's descriptive plot line (exegetical idea) with its message/theology. Typically, this results in a "When you are in a situation similar to the one in the biblical story, God will respond to you pretty much the same way he responded to them" hermeneutic.

Most of what's wrong with this approach has already been discussed. Here, however, I want to address the idea that when we are in a situation "similar" to that in a narrative, we will get "similar" results. Here is an exegetical idea (EI) and THT from a careful practitioner of this approach:

> EI: When <u>David</u> failed to walk with God, <u>he</u> put <u>his</u> life, family, and career in jeopardy.

> THT: When <u>believers</u> fail to walk with God, <u>they</u> put <u>their</u> lives, families, and careers in jeopardy.[15]

---

15. See Mathewson, *The Art of Preaching Old Testament Narrative*, 106. Mathewson's "theological [big] idea" is functionally similar to the THT.

Notice the specificity of results: "they put their lives, families, and careers in jeopardy." It's too specific. It asserts more than 2 Samuel 11–12 teaches. In the next chapter, we'll discuss how to determine the OTM and THT of OT narratives, and why "discipline" should be in those for 2 Samuel 11–12.

A study of the book of Judges demonstrates why we need to avoid such specificity. Seven times in Judges, Israel committed the same sin: doing "what was evil in the sight of the Lord" (2:11; 3:7; 3:12; 4:1; 6:1; 10:6; 13:1). God's responses—the results—included discipline each time, but the specifics of the discipline were unpredictably different. Commenting on this variety in Judges, Robert Chisholm writes:

> Though God is unchanging in his very essence, this does not mean that he always relates to people in the same way. . . . If we learn anything from the stories of the Old Testament, it is that God cannot be placed in a box where his response can be predicted. On the contrary, he is free to act as he pleases, even though his actions may seem contradictory or inconsistent from our limited perspective.[16]

I know that you want to preach with biblical authority. If you see room for improvement in your preaching, take heart. I know how vulnerable it makes us feel to recognize imperfections of such a personal nature. I know how scary it is to mess with the preaching methods that have gotten us where we are today. I get it. You have no reason to be disappointed or ashamed. God has worked through you and will continue to. It took courage to get you "here." Use that same courage to take you "there."

---

16. Chisholm, *Interpreting the Historical Books*, 191.

CHAPTER 2

OT NARRATIVES: FROM TEXT SELECTION TO TAKE-HOME TRUTH

Having provided an overview of what it takes to preach OT narratives with biblical authority, this chapter discusses the skills that make it possible. In working with pastors, I've found that these skills are not difficult to learn, but do take a few pages to explain. To shorten the learning curve, download and use the one-page OT Narrative worksheet found at http://www.preachingworks.com/worksheets.html. *Refer to it regularly as you read this chapter.* Since 2 Samuel 11–12 is used as an example throughout, it would also make sense to have that passage in front of you as you read.

Once you learn these skills, expect your preaching of OT narratives to be a richer experience. It may also be a more spiritual experience because it takes real trust in God and his Word to not shoot straight for easy misapplications. Having been subtly convinced that anything with a biblical flavor is good enough, it takes courage to preach God's message from OT narratives.

I am confident your listeners will appreciate the difference. There is a reason why more than forty percent of the Bible is narrative. People, by God's design, want to see how their personal narrative fits into a larger one. They want to fit into something bigger than their small world. Through OT narratives, God says, "I'm redeeming the world. Trust me, and you can be an active part of it."

Overview of the Steps

In **Step 1: Select a Complete Unit of Thought (CUT)**, we'll discuss how to select proper preaching texts. To preach OT narratives with biblical authority, we almost always need to preach entire CUTs.

In **Step 2: Identify the Theological and Historical Contexts**, we'll see that OT narratives are designed to teach something about God—his nature or covenant-keeping—to people who lived under a different covenant and, in some ways, had different felt needs. When the material in this step is ignored, our sermon's message and applications will likely veer in the wrong direction.

In **Step 3: Study the Plot**, we'll go over how to appreciate and grasp the intricate design of OT narratives. We'll also discuss the role and effective use of scholarly commentaries and reference works, so that we can preach more dynamic messages.

In **Step 4: Discover the Original-Theological Message (OTM)**, we'll discuss how to discern the primary theological message an OT narrative is designed to teach. Since it's possible for OTMs to be accurate, precise, and unhelpful, it will include practical advice on writing them well.

In **Step 5: Craft the Take-Home Truth (THT)**, we'll discuss how to turn OTMs into THTs, so that our sermons will proclaim and apply their texts' messages in ways that today's listeners can understand.

The question everyone asks me is: How long will all of this take? The answer: three to five hours. Most of that time will be in

Step 3, where we'll ask good questions and get good answers. The steps in this chapter, however, are only part of sermon preparation. Part II of the book discusses the rest of it. We need to accept that quality, full-length sermons take about fifteen hours to prepare. A quality sermon is no less than one that accurately proclaims and applies the message of its preaching text(s) and is so easy to follow that one hour after church most listeners could tell us the THT or main points from memory (even if it's in their own words).

Step 1:
Select a Complete Unit of Thought

Preaching OT narratives with biblical authority requires careful text selection. A poorly chosen preaching text can doom the sermon before it begins. In general, we need to preach an entire CUT, because OT narratives teach few theological principles and because it takes an entire CUT to convey an OTM. Thus, preaching partial CUTs typically results in misapplication.

Nonetheless, there are a few instances in which it's possible to select a preaching text and discern a legitimate OTM from a passage that's smaller than a CUT. Genesis 11:27–12:9 is a good example. These verses form a CUT that consists of a genealogy in 11:27–32 and a narrative in 12:1–9 that begins in vv. 1–3 with a covenantal declaration. The nature of 12:1–3 makes it legitimate to preach from only those verses. Preachers could also choose to preach from 12:1–9 without making explicit reference to 11:27–32, although it would be a good idea to include any contribution those verses make to the CUT's context or theological message in the Set the Stage portion of the introduction (more about this in chapter 5).

Some preachers who are committed to the idea that no CUT should be skipped when preaching through a book, but are also concerned that preaching one CUT at a time will take too long, seek to preach two or more CUTs at a time. This is a legitimate option, but I advise strongly against it. It makes it difficult to preach with excellence. This is because excellent sermons do more than "tell" listeners about the text and its theology. They "show." They preach through the text in a clear, unified way that enables listeners to see and feel the text's dynamics and theology in the text for themselves. Thus, authority resides in the text, not the preacher.

What is it about preaching multiple CUTs in the same sermon that makes this difficult? It's their emotional-dramatic arcs and their length. Each OT narrative has its own emotional-dramatic arc. Given their length, usually the only way to preach through multiple ones is to fail to convey the individual arcs. Even if in some cases it is possible, choosing this option serves the preacher's need to preach through the book quickly, not the listeners. Listeners enjoy going through most biblical books one CUT at a time, as long as it's done well. Nonetheless, if you sense the need to finish a book in a shorter period of time, then skip a few CUTs along the way, as long as you don't do it out of ulterior motives (e.g., desire to appease listeners by avoiding difficult or challenging passages).

Old Testament narratives contain three clues to help us identify where their CUTs begin and end: (1) a complete plot, (2) beginning markers, and (3) end markers. Since the identification of a CUT is not an exact science, the greater the number of indicators, the more certain is our identification.

Complete Plot

Biblical narratives usually contain four plot stages: introduction, problem, solution, and conclusion.[1] The introduction stage provides the story's setting. The problem stage starts when narration of the CUT's major plot conflict begins and ends when that conflict reaches its highest intensity. The solution stage begins the moment

---

1. Over time, you may want to learn the more detailed approach presented in Longman, *Literary Approaches to Biblical Interpretation*, 92. You can learn it by preparing sermons with the help of Greidanus, *Preaching Christ from Genesis* and *Preaching Christ from Daniel*.

a character appears or an action occurs that will eventually resolve the major plot conflict, and ends when it's fully resolved. The conclusion stage provides the outcome and finishes the story.

In 2 Samuel 11–12, 11:1 serves as the introduction, alerting us to the story's main character, location, and time of year. The problem stage begins at 11:2 and reaches its peak at 11:27. If the narrative ended at 11:27, readers would be left disappointed and appalled that David got away with murder. The solution stage begins at 12:1, where God intervenes unexpectedly via Nathan the prophet. The solution stage ends at 12:25, where David and Bathsheba's child dies. The conclusion covers 12:26–31, which details the birth of Solomon and Israel's success in battle.

Beginning and End Markers

Old Testament narratives often provide objective beginning and end markers to help readers identify CUTs. These markers are helpful because our sense of where a complete plot begins and ends can be quite subjective. Therefore, rely more on beginning and end markers to establish or confirm our sense of where a CUT begins and ends.

The most common beginning markers are:

1. Introductions to new main characters
   - "Now Absalom, David's son, had a beautiful sister, whose name was Tamar. And after a time, Amnon, David's son, loved her" (2 Sam. 13:1).
2. Introductions to a change of time
   - "In the spring of the year, the time when kings go out to battle" (2 Sam. 11:1).
3. Introductions to a change in place
   - "After the death of Saul, when David had returned from striking down the Amalekites, David remained two days in Ziklag" (2 Sam. 1:1).
4. Phrases that a book frequently uses to begin a narrative
   - In 2 Samuel, "After this" opens five CUTs.

The most common end markers are:

1. Concluding statements
   - "Then David and all the people returned to Jerusalem" (2 Sam. 12:31c).
2. Concluding summaries
   - "So Mephibosheth ate at David's table, like one of the king's sons. And Mephibosheth had a young son, whose name was Mica. And all who lived in Ziba's house became Mephibosheth's servants. So Mephibosheth lived in Jerusalem, for he ate always at the king's table. Now he was lame in both his feet" (2 Sam. 9:11b–13).

We need to also look at the beginning and end markers of the surrounding narratives. For example, even when a CUT does not have a clear beginning marker, we can still know where it begins by noticing the clear end marker in the previous narrative.

Step 2:
Identify the Theological and Historical Contexts

Once a CUT has been identified, the search for its OTM begins. What you'll see in this section is that OT narratives are designed to teach something about God—his nature or covenant-keeping. Therefore, our goal in Steps 2 through 4 is to ask and answer:

> **What question is this CUT designed to answer about God—his nature or covenant-keeping—to ancient Israel?**

Theological Context
Old Testament narratives are designed to teach something about God—his nature or covenant-keeping. This is true of narrative CUTs that never mention God, such as 2 Samuel 13 or those in

the book of Esther. Andrew Hill and John Walton write, "Think of the [OT narrative] books as theological. . . . Remember that the main focus . . . . is God and his covenant, not people or events."[2] They add:

> The purpose of the historical literature . . . is to show the ways in which the Lord has acted in history to fulfill his covenant promises and to carry out his agenda. One could call it didactic (giving instruction) in the sense that it is revelation of who God is by recording what he has done. . . . Some readers are inclined to look for new insights and lessons in each account. But rather . . . [look for] patterns, themes, and motifs that we ought to see as weaving the historical tapestry into a picture of the sovereign God of the covenant. The significance of each thread is the contribution it makes to the tapestry. . . . The narratives must be approached through their context, and God must be seen as the focus."[3]

Peter Vogt writes:

> We must also bear in mind that biblical narratives usually have a theological[4] purpose. That is, the authors were less interested in conveying details about the lives of even the biblical "heroes" than in communicating something about God and his interaction with his people. In Genesis 39, the emphasis is not on Joseph per se but on God's faithfulness in being with Joseph . . . *in order to accomplish his purposes in the lives of the descendants of Abraham.*[5]

---

2. Hill and Walton, *A Survey of the Old Testament*, 211.
3. Ibid., 211–12.
4. Scholars often contrast the terms "theological" and "ethical" in their discussions of OT narrative. Old Testament narratives are theological in the sense that their messages are about God and generally don't prescribe specific human behaviors (ethics).
5. Vogt, *Interpreting the Pentateuch*, 51 (emphasis added).

The God-centered focus of OT narratives does not mean that they are not intended to influence human behavior. On the contrary, they are written to affectively teach something about God—his nature or covenant-keeping—so that people will trust him in every area of life. In other words, OT narratives are about God, but they are intended to transform us. Yaira Amit puts it this way:

> It seems reasonable to assume that the authors of biblical narratives believed that if they told their flock about God's mighty deeds—how God saved the people in times of distress, how their fate was in God's hands, and how it paid to obey God—then the community of worshipers would keep its side of the covenant and remain faithful to God."[6]

Historical Context

Old Testament narratives teach something about God—his nature or covenant-keeping—but they do so within an Old Covenant context. In order to preach them well, we need to read them in light of (1) ancient Israel's view of the retribution principle and afterlife, (2) their latest Old Covenant expansion, and (3) their original audience.

Ancient Israel's View of the Retribution Principle and Afterlife

The Old Covenant operates on the basis of the retribution principle. The retribution principle teaches that God will bless those who follow him and curse those who do not. It is found in Genesis 12:1–3 and is expressed in different ways throughout the OT (e.g., Deut. 28, and applied in different ways throughout the prophets).

The retribution principle sounds straightforward enough until we realize that Israel expected it to be carried out in this life. This is because Israel had no concept of *reward* or *punishment* in the afterlife until the book of Daniel, one of the latest books of the OT.[7]

---

6. Amit, *Reading Biblical Narratives*, 2.
7. Buis, *Zondervan Encyclopedia of the Bible*, s.v. "Retribution." See also Walton, *Dictionary of the Old Testament: Wisdom, Poetry, & Writings*, s.v. "Retribution"; Dallaire, "Judaism and the World to Come," 37–60.

Israel's view of the retribution principle and afterlife explains many things about the OT: why Job's friends stubbornly insisted on his guilt; why the psalmists expressed thoroughgoing distress and expected that God would rescue them in the here and now; why Proverbs is so optimistic; and why Ecclesiastes helps put the optimism of Proverbs into perspective. *For preaching OT narratives, we need to be aware that Israel's military victories are a sign of God's blessing resulting from the king's or Israel's obedience.*[8]

Israel's insistence that God carry out the retribution principle in this life was neither a selfish, prideful, nor immature demand—as it might be today. Since Israel was unaware of reward or punishment in the afterlife, God's honor was at stake if he didn't act in the here and now, because he would appear to be as fickle as the gods of the surrounding nations.

Latest Old Covenant Expansion

The Old Covenant is the foundation of the OT. Succinctly expressed in Genesis 12:1–3, the scope of the Old Covenant was expanded to include:

- Eden (Gen. 3:15)
- Noah (Gen. 9:8–17)
- Abraham (Gen. 12:1–3)
  - → The Promised Land (Gen. 15)
  - → Circumcision (Gen. 17:1–14)
- Law (Exod. 19:5–6; 20–23; Deut., esp. 1:7–8; 7:7–10; 9:4–6; 28)
- David (2 Sam. 7:8–16; 1 Kings 2:1–4; 6:12–13; 9:4–9; 11:11–13, 32–39)

It is crucial to be aware—from the vantage point of the preaching text—of the most recent Old Covenant expansion. For example,

---

8. For further explanation, see Walton and Hill, *Old Testament Today*, 326–28, 336–38, 344–46, 352–57, 361–66.

2 Samuel 11–12 must be read in light of 7:8–16. Likewise, 1 Kings 15 must be understood in light of not just 2 Samuel 7:8–16, but also the conditional way it is expressed in 1 Kings 2–11.

One way to tell if an OT narrative is primarily about God's nature or God's covenant-keeping is to notice whether it refers to, or fulfills, any part of the CUT's latest Old Covenant expansion. One way we can know that 2 Samuel 11–12 pertains to God's covenant-keeping is because Solomon's birth fulfills the next step of the Davidic Covenant (2 Sam. 7:8–16), that narrative's latest Old Covenant expansion.

Original Audience

Biblical narratives were not written for those in them. Neither were they written *directly* to us. They were written to address the situation of their original audiences. Interpretations that ignore the historical situation of the original audience are likely to be incorrect. Klein, Blomberg, and Hubbard state, "Any appraisal of 'meaning,' then, must take into consideration this complex coalition of text, author, and audience. . . . Knowing all the conditions that surround the recipients of the original message provides further insight into how they most likely understood the message."[9] Haddon Robinson puts it this way: "I cannot make [a] passage mean something today that it did not mean in principle in the ancient world. . . . I have to be honest with the text before I can come over to the contemporary world."[10]

Reading OT narratives with the original audience in mind helps us avoid reinterpreting their messages to reflect our agenda (*eisegesis*). For example, realizing that Israel already had a moral code, the Law, should help us realize that OT narratives were probably not designed to be handbooks of moral principles.

Old Testament narratives were originally composed for one of three audiences: Israel preparing to do battle for the Promised Land, Israel in the Promised Land, or Israel under foreign

---

9. Klein, Blomberg, and Hubbard, *Introduction to Biblical Interpretation*, 9–11.
10. Robinson, "The Heresy of Application," 308.

domination. Books with original composition dates before 1200 BC were written to Israel preparing to do battle for the Promised Land; those with dates between 1200 and 586 BC were written to Israel in the Promised Land; those with dates after 586 BC were written to Israel under foreign domination.

Israel preparing to enter the Promised Land needed assurance that their one God would do what they'd been told he'd do: give them victory over the numerous gods and armies that occupied the Promised Land. In their world, the idea of trusting in one God was crazy. They needed assurance that their God would do what he said he would do.[11]

Israel in the Promised Land needed to know how to survive and, preferably, thrive as a nation in the Promised Land. These weren't dumb people. In 1–2 Samuel, we discover that they were realists. They believed that God is great, but also considered a king necessary for their security (1 Sam 8:19–20). Apparently, two of their biggest enemies thought the same way. In Daniel 3:15b, Nebuchadnezzar, king of Babylon, asks Shadrach, Meshach, and Abednego, "And who is the god who will deliver you out of my hands?"[12] In Isaiah 36:18–20, Sennacherib, king of Assyria, told Israel to

> beware lest [your King] Hezekiah mislead you by saying, "The LORD will deliver us." Has any of the gods of the nations delivered his land out of the king of Assyria? Where are the gods of Hamath and Arpad? Where are the gods of Sepharvaim? Have they delivered Samaria out of my hand? Who among all the gods of these lands have delivered their lands out of my hand, that the LORD should deliver Jerusalem out of my hand?

Israel under foreign domination needed to know: What is God doing? How sovereign is God? Why should we trust God? For

---

11. For a fascinating survey of why idolatry was, and is, so tempting, see Stuart, "The Attractions of Idolatry," in *Exodus*, 450–53.
12. What question do you think this narrative is designed to answer? Cf. vv. 28–29 later in the chapter.

example, notice how the book of Daniel immediately addresses questions like these: "In the third year of the reign of Jehoiakim king of Judah, Nebuchadnezzar king of Babylon came to Jerusalem and besieged it. *And the Lord gave* Jehoiakim king of Judah into his hand, with some of the vessels of the house of God" (1:1–2).

Step 3:
Study the Plot

Preparing sermons from OT narratives requires a thoughtful study of plot. We must know the ins and outs of our preaching text(s) to proclaim them well. If these skills are relatively new to you, expect to find that practicing them will take your enjoyment of OT narratives to new heights. It's when we discover the intricate design of OT narratives that we come to appreciate their beauty and power.

While a good portion of what's discovered will not make it into your sermon, it will all benefit it. It will infuse you with enthusiasm, empower you to recreate the text's dynamics, and help you develop an effective sermon structure.

Bo Mathews understood this. Not one to produce "information dumping" sermons, he was asked once, "Why do you spend as much time and strength on your sermons as you do?" He replied, "That half hour on Sunday morning represents the one time that I have the most exposure to my people. I think it warrants every piece of energy I invest in it. . . . I think people need it and deserve it."[13]

As you work through this step, keep asking:

> **What question is this CUT designed to answer about God—his nature or covenant-keeping—to ancient Israel?**

Before we go further, be aware that sooner or later you will find yourself doing Steps 3 and 4 simultaneously.

---

13. Matthews, "He Who Has Ears to Hear . . . Jeremiah 1," 130.

Write Scene Summaries

Old Testament CUTs usually cover one to two chapters, so begin your study of plot by typing out brief summaries of each scene. This is sermon preparation, not a research paper. Don't worry about misidentifying where a scene begins and ends. For now, only strive to make your scene summaries clear enough to remind you of the narrative's plot. Guaranteed, our initial drafts will have mistakes. That's okay. We're ten minutes into sermon preparation! Here are sample scene summaries for 2 Samuel 11–12:

> (11:1–5) When kings go off to war, David stays behind, and sends Joab and Israel's army out to battle. They besiege Rabbah. Back at the palace, David sees Bathsheba and has messengers get her. He sleeps with her, and she gets pregnant.
>
> (11:6–25) David calls for Uriah. When Uriah comes, David twice tries to get Uriah to sleep with Bathsheba. When Uriah doesn't, David tells Joab to put Uriah at the battlefront to die. Joab does, and Uriah dies.
>
> (11:26–27) Bathsheba mourns. David marries her.
>
> (12:1–14) God sends Nathan to David. Via Nathan, God "sets up" David with a parable. David incriminates himself. David is told he's the parable's guilty person. Since God gave everything to David and David despised God's word, David will be disciplined. David repents, and God forgives him, but David's pre-born child will die.
>
> (12:15–23) David fasts and pleads with God to save the child. On the seventh day, the child dies. The servants don't want to tell David the child died, but David picks up on their behavior and discovers the child's death. David, then, worships God and begins to eat again, confusing his servants.

(12:24–25) David comforts Bathsheba. She conceives another child. Solomon is born. The LORD loves Solomon.

(12:26–31) Joab captures most of Rabbah. Joab calls David and tells him to join him to take the rest of the city, or else Joab will name the city after himself upon capturing it. David joins the battle. Rabbah is captured, plundered, and subjugated. David and Israel return home.

Scene summaries have two benefits. First, they help us to quickly see how an insight we discover while studying one scene fits into the narrative as a whole. Second, scene summaries—in their revised form—can morph into our sermon's "movements." Movements are like main points in that they (1) give our sermons shape, (2) summarize the texts they refer to, and (3) are best spoken immediately prior to reading the texts they encapsulate. I call them "movements" instead of "main points," because they are descriptive (often multi-sentence) summaries. Main points—as I define them—are single, application-oriented sentences. Notice the difference:

Movement: **As the story opens, we find David in his palace and David's entire army in battle.** Read with me [2 Samuel 11,] verse 1 …

Main Point: **What I want us to see is that God blesses those who consistently follow him.** [restate]
Read with me [Psalm 1,] verses 1 & 2 …

Identify Main Characters

Identifying main characters is important because it clues us in to who the biblical author considers to be the story's major players. In OT narratives, we can tell who they are by counting proper names (e.g., the LORD, David, Bathsheba, Uriah). The key is to count only the number of times a character's proper name appears, even if it's used to refer to someone else (e.g., "Uriah's wife" counts toward Uriah, not Bathsheba). Furthermore, don't count titles (e.g., king, husband, wife), pronouns (e.g., he, she, him, her, they), or gender references (e.g., woman, man). Keep in mind that when a group acts in unison, that group counts as a single character. For example, in Judges 18 the proper name "Dan" refers to the Israelite tribe of Dan. Since the tribe of Dan acts in unison—even when represented by five leaders—and its proper name appears thirteen times, Dan is both a single character and a main character.

In 2 Samuel 11–12, one way we can tell that its plot has little to do with adultery is by noticing that Bathsheba is a minor character, as she is named only twice. David, however, is named forty-one times, Uriah twenty-three, the LORD fourteen, and Joab thirteen. In Judges 18, a character is identified thirteen times, eleven as "priest," twice as "Levite," but never by his proper name. If the narrative's main characters, Dan and Micah, are named twelve to thirteen times, shouldn't the priest/Levite be considered a main character? The answer is no. Refusing to identify the priest/Levite by name is the biblical author's way of letting us know that, for narrative purposes, he is more like an object that is fought over than a person.

In OT narrative, God is always a main character, even when he is absent, because he is the controlling player. In fact, the longer he is absent from a narrative CUT or book, the more we should inquire into what he's up to. In 2 Samuel 13, does God's absence indicate that he is not a main character or that the narrative is not about him? Nope. The story's events are a direct result of the discipline that God announced via Nathan in the previous story.

There are a number of ways to count proper names. If you have Bible software, use it. Here's another way: When you read through a CUT early in sermon preparation, write down each proper name the first time you notice it. Then, pull up the passage at Bible Gateway (http://www.biblegateway.com) and use your browser's "find" option to count proper names. Will this always give you the exact number of times that a proper name appears in the Hebrew text of that CUT? No, but the exact number isn't necessary.

Find Out What the Narrative Dwells On

Old Testament narratives are famous for their economy of words. We may find them long—some take ten minutes to read—but all things considered, they are brief. Very brief. Every word is carefully chosen. Every scene is intentionally proportioned. Discovering what the narrative dwells on is important for discerning what's most important in a narrative's plot and theology (see Step 4 for its usefulness to theology).

Using the one-page worksheet, break the CUT into its major scenes. Don't stress over hyper-precision; even scholars can disagree on scene divisions. For each scene, (1) note how many verses the scene occupies, (2) estimate how long the events in the scene took in real life, and (3) estimate what percentage of the scene is dialogue. Here are the results for 2 Samuel 11–12:

Find Out What the Narrative Dwells On (2 Samuel 11–12)

Major Scenes	# of vv.	Real Time (est.)	Dialogue (est.)	Scene Description
11:1–5	5	60 days	13%	Intro, David's adultery, pregnancy
11:6–25	20	30 days	50%	David's murder of Uriah
11:26–27	2	210 days	0%	Bathsheba's mourning, remarriage, birth
12:1–14	14	1 hour	90%	God's rebuke of David via Nathan
12:15–23	9	7 days	40%	God's discipline via child's death
12:24–25	2	270 days	0%	Birth of Solomon
12:26–31	6	60 days	20%	Military victory

The plot's most important scenes are those (1) with the highest concentration of dialogue, (2) that are the longest, and (3) with the highest ratio of narrated time to real time—i.e., the largest number of verses per day that the scene took to occur in real life.

In 2 Samuel 11–12, it may surprise us to learn that God's rebuke of David via Nathan in 12:1–14 is the most important scene. We can know this because it has the highest concentration of dialogue, the highest ratio of narrated time to real time (fourteen verses for one hour!), and is the second-longest scene. We discover that David's murder of Uriah in 11:6–25—which exemplifies God's charges against David in 12:7–14—is the second most important scene because it is the longest, has the second highest concentration of dialogue, and has the second highest ratio of narrated time to real time.

Ask Good Questions and Get Good Answers

One of the most misunderstood concepts of sermon preparation is the idea of "doing our own work." The problem isn't with the idea, but our understanding of it. Too often we take it to mean that we should study the text on our own and not "depend" on commentaries. That sounds so noble until we realize that this misunderstanding is the surest way for most of us to preach our thoughts as if they were God's.

The concept of "doing your own work" really means this: *Do the work you are qualified to do, but verify and supplement it with high-quality reference works*. Notice that there is no "then" in the preceding sentence. There is nothing—including the Bible—that suggests we don't need or shouldn't use commentaries and other reference works throughout sermon preparation.

There is no shame in being honest about our abilities. As Paul says, "I say to everyone among you not to think of himself more highly than he ought to think, but to think with sober judgment" (Rom. 12:3). Failure is not making frequent use of competent reference works. It's misrepresenting our Wholly Other God and his Word when we didn't have to. We should never underestimate our ability to misrepresent God *in the pulpit*.

The other mistake we make is to prepare sermons with the help of others who are no more qualified than we are. Since preaching today—whether verse-by-verse or topical, seeker-friendly or seeker-*un*friendly, fundamentalist or emergent—is largely our thoughts with biblical flavoring added, many of us look to creative and successful preachers to help us "use" God's Word effectively. If God "blessed" their "use" of Scripture, it has to be good enough, right?

There is a humble and happy medium: Ask lots of good questions throughout the CUT—even when you think you know the answers—and get good answers from people who are specialists in their fields. A key phrase here is "even when you think you know the answers." I've trained enough pastors to know that we are way too quick to assume that our interpretations are accurate. Are specialists always right? Of course not, but they know a lot more about our preaching texts than we do.

I find it interesting that when pastors start taking a question-based approach to commentary work, they learn to enjoy using scholarly commentaries. One day, I shared this with my wife Sara, who is a professor of reading. She replied, "That makes perfect sense. Reading non-fiction is much more enjoyable when you have a purpose for reading it. Going to technical commentaries with only the vaguest hope of getting something out of them would disillusion anyone. By going to commentaries to get *their* questions answered, pastors find meaning and purpose in it. Some probably think it's fun."

As you ask questions, feel free to draw your own *provisional* conclusions, but verify their accuracy. Get excited when you find out your provisional conclusions are wrong! And guess what? For a (potentially long) while you may find they are frequently wrong. That's okay. We're preachers. We're not called to know everything about a passage the first time we read it. We're called to get it right when we preach it.

What questions should we ask of OT narratives? Any question that helps us understand their background, design, or intent. Here are some examples:

- What's going on in this section of the book?
- Who is/are . . . ? What is the reader expected to know about them?
- What does . . . mean in this context?
- Why is this detail included at this point?
- What purpose does . . . serve in the narrative?
- Why did the character say or do . . . ? Was this expected/acceptable behavior at that time?
- What might be the original audience's visceral reaction to this?
- If this means . . . , how does it fit with [another part of the CUT, book, or Bible]?

A good way to do this is to write or type your questions in two columns—one for verse references, the other for the questions themselves—and then note your answers as you search through your resources. Since these lists are for you, make them work for you. Don't worry about writing them out as grammatically correct sentences. Feel free to not list sub-questions as I do below, if the main question will remind you of them. Furthermore, *add questions based on what's discussed in Steps 1, 2, and 4*:

Asking Good Questions of 2 Samuel 11:1–3	
vv.	Question
1	When is the "spring of the year"?
1	What does it mean that it's the time of year that "kings go out to battle"? • Does every king in the area go out to battle? • Is this just another way of saying that the spring is "battle season"? • Do the actual kings go to battle or is the king still considered as having gone to battle if his army went, but he didn't? • Why would the narrator have to mention that "the spring of the year" is "the time when kings go out to battle"? Wouldn't the original audience already know that?

vv.	Asking Good Questions of 2 Samuel 11:1–3
	Question
1	What does "all Israel" mean? • Is it correct to say that it doesn't include women and children? • Is it another way of saying, "nearly all able-bodied men"?
1	Who are the Ammonites? • What is Israel's past history with them?
1	Where is Rabbah? • Is Rabbah an Ammonite town?
1	What am I expected to get out of the fact that "David remained at Jerusalem"?
2	Does "arose" mean that David was sleeping in the afternoon? If David took a nap, did everyone take a nap in the afternoon? • Just the rich? Just the king?
2	Why was the woman [Bathsheba] bathing on the roof? • Was this common or acceptable behavior?
2	Why are we told that the woman "was very beautiful"?
3	Why does it say that David "sent and inquired" about Bathsheba? • What is the significance of "sent" in this context?
3	The beginning of the verse makes it seem like David didn't know who the woman was, but the response he got makes it seem like he did know and just wanted confirmation. Did he know who she was or not?
3	What does the narrator expect me to know about Eliam?
3	Why are we told that Uriah is a Hittite? • Who are the Hittites? • What is a Hittite doing in Israel, much less Israel's army?

This skill requires patience. Like the skill of listening effectively to our kids, we must put other things out of our minds, give our full attention to it, and accept that it will take longer than we want to give it. Expect to dedicate thirty to sixty minutes to simply asking questions of the CUT.

Select Quality Reference Works

We are the reference works we use. Our choice of resources affect the accuracy and quality of our sermons. What follows are my minimum recommendations.

Begin by spending about twelve dollars to purchase the latest edition of Tremper Longman's *Old Testament Commentary Survey*, and prepare sermons with at least five of his top picks. Using five commentaries is helpful to ensure you get most or all of your questions answered. For example, your questions about the literary dynamics of a passage are not likely to be answered by a commentary that focuses on historical issues. Further, using five commentaries allows you to consider multiple views on most issues, which is especially important if a scholar advocates for an interpretation so ingenious that no other scholar finds it plausible—for good reasons. Unless there is a compelling reason, if Longman doesn't mention a commentary or rates it poorly, don't use it.

Additionally, I recommend having the latest editions of the following reference works handy throughout sermon preparation:

- *A Survey of the Old Testament* by Andrew E. Hill and John H. Walton
- *An Introduction to the Old Testament* by Tremper Longman III and Raymond B. Dillard
- Two of the following:
  → *The Zondervan Encyclopedia of the Bible* by Merrill C. Tenney and Moisés Silva, eds.
  → *The Baker Illustrated Bible Dictionary* by Tremper Longman III, et al., eds.
  → *The International Standard Bible Encyclopedia* by Geoffrey W. Bromiley, ed.
  → *Dictionary of the Old Testament: Pentateuch* by Desmond T. Alexander and David W. Baker, eds.
  → *Dictionary of the Old Testament: Historical Books* by Bill T. Arnold and H. G. M. Williamson, eds.
  → *Dictionary of the Old Testament: Wisdom, Poetry, & Writings* by Tremper Longman III and Peter Enns, eds.

- One of the following:
  → *New Bible Commentary* by D. A. Carson, et al., eds.
  → *The Baker Illustrated Bible Commentary* by Gary M. Burge and Andrew E. Hill, eds.

Of course, feel free to use more advanced works like *The Hebrew and Aramaic Lexicon of the Old Testament* (HALOT). However, the reference works above should suffice for sermon preparation.

I recommend you have an assistant or volunteer photocopy and staple together the pages of each commentary that relate to your preaching text, so you don't have to fumble through these bulky tomes. It will make it much faster and easier to look through each one to get answers to your questions.

You might be wondering about the role of Bible software. If you are proficient at BibleWorks or Logos, use it. I use Logos, and many of the reference works mentioned above are available in it. The biggest problem with Bible software is that the vast majority of the resources in their packages are junk or outdated and should be avoided—seriously. Some also find that these excess resources slow down the software. The first thing I do when I upgrade to a new package is uninstall (or avoid installing) virtually everything that comes with it, except for any top-notch reference works. There's usually a good reason, related to the credibility of the work, for why the best works don't often come with a package and must be purchased individually.

Step 4:
Determine the Original-Theological Message

We now turn to skills for discerning the *wording* of an OT narrative's OTM. The OTM is the primary theological principle that a CUT was designed to communicate to its original audience. As we discussed in Step 2, arriving at an OTM requires that we discover and answer:

What question is this CUT designed to answer about God—his nature or covenant-keeping—to ancient Israel?

Since OT narratives are about God, the grammatical subject of their OTMs will be "God" or "the LORD." It's helpful to discover not just the OTM, but also the question it answers because it will likely morph into the question in the sermon's Focus. The question 2 Samuel 11–12 answers is, "What kind of sinful king of Israel will God use to fulfill the Davidic Covenant?"

To determine the *wording* of an OT narrative's OTM, we must engage in theological analysis of (1) structural commentary, (2) characters, and (3) each scene. When studying each of these, the key question to answer is:

What is the theological or literary contribution of this aspect of the narrative?

For the purposes of this step, a portion of a narrative makes a theological contribution when it contributes to the message of the CUT. As we discussed in chapter 1, OT narratives may teach a small number of ancillary theological principles in addition to the primary one, but this step is concerned only with the primary theological principle.

Thus, once we discover that a portion of a narrative makes a theological contribution, we need to then discern if it's primary or ancillary. As we've discussed, 2 Samuel 11:27b—working together with 11:4–25—makes an ancillary theological contribution to the CUT: Murder is wrong, even for the king. Nonetheless, that won't make it into the OTM.

However, it would be a mistake to envision an impenetrable wall between the theological and the literary. Anything that contributes to an OTM's *wording* also makes a literary contribution. For example, God's confrontation of David via Nathan in 2 Samuel 12:7–14 makes a significant contribution to both the OTM and the plot—it's a dramatic confrontation! Likewise, David's murder of Uriah in 11:6–25 makes a significant literary contribution, but it also supports and exemplifies much of the OTM. It's all one narrative, but certain aspects of it are intended to contribute to the way readers could, if they wanted to, express its message in a straightforward manner.

Theological Analysis of Structural Commentary.
The first thing to analyze to determine the *wording* of an OT narrative's OTM is structural commentary. Structural commentary includes (1) genre, (2) previous CUTs, (3) comments by the narrator, and (4) repeated words or phrases. Genre was discussed in Step 2 and informs us that the OTM pertains to God's nature or covenant-keeping. The discussion here, therefore, will be on the latter three.

Previous CUTs
Periodically, CUTs of OT narrative are designed to be read with one or more previous CUTs at the *forefront* of our minds. This is because their plots unfold similarly or address similar theological issues. For example, we know that Abraham's and Isaac's "my sister" narratives in Genesis 12:10–20, 20:1–18, and 26:1–35 are designed to be read in light of each other because their plots unfold very similarly. We know that 2 Samuel 11–12 is designed to be read in light of 1 Samuel 13 and 15—where God rejects King Saul for seemingly lesser offenses—because they both deal with God's (un)willingness to use sinful kings of Israel.

Perceiving when a CUT should be read explicitly in light of another can help us determine the specific question it answers about God's nature or God's covenant-keeping. For example, knowing that 2 Samuel 11–12 should be read in light of 1 Samuel 13 and 15 helps us realize that its OTM will answer a question about the kind of king that God will or won't use to fulfill the David Covenant (2 Sam 7:8–16)—the CUT's latest Old Covenant expansion.

To pick up on the significance of previous CUTs, it's usually necessary to check with scholarly commentaries, particularly those that focus on literary and theological matters. It was David Firth's commentary, for example, that alerted me to the connection between 2 Samuel 11–12 and 1 Samuel 13 and 15.[14]

---

14. Firth, *1 & 2 Samuel*, 430–31.

Comments by the Narrator

In biblical narratives, the narrator is the person telling the story. With rare exceptions, narrators stand above the action, relating events from God's omniscient perspective. Biblical narrators tend to refrain from making explicit comments, preferring to allow characters and events to speak for themselves. In 2 Samuel 13, for example, the narrator doesn't feel the need to comment on the sinfulness of Amnon's rape of Tamar. The audience is expected to be horrified by it.

When narrators do comment, however, it's usually to either explain or evaluate something important.[15] The comment in 11:4, for example, is a parenthetical explanation: "Now she [Bathsheba] had been purifying herself from her uncleanness."[16] The comment in 11:27 is evaluative: "But the thing that David had done displeased the LORD."[17]

What is the theological or literary contribution of this aspect of the narrative?	
Narrator Comment	Theological or Literary Contribution
"Now she [Bathsheba] had been purifying herself from her uncleanness" (2 Sam 11:4b).	LITERARY: The narrator is making the crucial point that Bathsheba wasn't pregnant when David lay with her.
"But the thing that David had done displeased the LORD" (2 Sam 11:27b).	THEOLOGICAL (ANCILLARY): After allowing the original audience to ponder whether the king—unlike them—can use legal means to murder someone, the narrator's answer is no. This comment also informs readers that God saw what happened, that he is displeased, and that they can expect him to intervene.

---

15. Bar-Efrat, *Narrative Art in the Bible*, 23–32.
16. Youngblood, "2 Samuel," 431.
17. Wenham, *Story as Torah*, 14.

Repeated Words or Phrases

In individual OT narratives or a series of them, there are often certain words that appear with far greater frequency than they do in the rest of the book. In 2 Samuel 10–12, for example, *šlḥ* (to send) appears twenty-three times. Scholarly commentaries will alert us to repeated key words or phrases, although instead of referring to them as key words or phrases, they may use *leitwort* to refer to key words and *leitmotiv* for key phrases.

Once we've discovered any *leitwort* or *leitmotiv*, it's time to ask, "What is the theological or literary contribution of this aspect of the narrative?" Often their contribution is literary, in that they heighten interest in the story. When they're included in dialogue, there is an increased chance that they will contribute to the *wording* of the OTM.

What is the theological or literary contribution of this aspect of the narrative?	
Repeated Words or Phrases	Theological or Literary Contribution
šlḥ (to send)	LITERARY: The repeated use of this word helps readers feel the authority and power of the "senders"—human and divine—to declare and actualize what they send.
mwt (to die)	LITERARY: The repeated use of this word helps readers feel for the powerless, whose "ever-present potential fate" is in the hands of the senders.[18]

Theological Analysis of Characters

The second skill for determining the *wording* of an OT narrative's OTM involves figuring out which characters are theologically representative and what they represent. While OT narratives are full of characters, usually only one or two make a contribution to the *wording* of

---

18. Youngblood, "2 Samuel," 432.

the OTM. Of the ten-plus characters in 2 Samuel 11–12, for example, only the LORD and David are theologically representative in the OTM. Since God is a main character in every OT narrative, even when he is absent, and since OT narratives are about him, God is theologically representative in every narrative. And, as you would expect, God is representative of himself. So then, "God" or "the LORD" will appear as the grammatical subject of every OT narrative OTM.

Theologically representative human characters, however, do not represent themselves in the OTM. In 2 Samuel 11–12, for example, David is not representative of himself, but of "kings of Israel." In Genesis 22:1–19, Isaac is representative of Israel. In Daniel 3, Babylon's king Nebuchadnezzar represents nations or world powers that set themselves up against God's rule or persecute those who trust in God.

Keep in mind, a character (e.g., Abraham) may be theologically representative in one narrative, but not in another. In Genesis 11:27–12:9, for example, Abraham is theologically representative of Israel. In Genesis 22:1–19, Abraham is not theologically representative in the OTM.[19] Furthermore, what a character represents in one narrative may not be what he represents in another narrative.

As we'll see in Step 5, it's crucial to put in the OTM what a character represents theologically, not the character's name. Those who treat OT narrative exegetical ideas as if they were OTMs frequently run afoul here. For example, using "David" instead of "kings of Israel" may lead us to mistakenly think that "David" can be replaced in the THT with "husband," "father," "leader," "believer," or "person."[20] While it is legitimate—in 2 Samuel 11–12 at least—to equate "kings of Israel" and "believers," these other "equivalents" are suspect.

Theological Analysis of Each Scene

The final skill for determining the *wording* of an OT narrative's OTM involves going through each scene to discern its contribution to the

---

19. See Greidanus, *Preaching Christ from Genesis*, 200; see also *Modern Preacher and the Ancient Text*, 179–81.
20. Mathewson, *The Art of Preaching Old Testament Narrative*, 86, 210.

wording of the OTM. I recommend analyzing each scene in their order of importance, as determined in Step 3. To do this, we look at each scene's dialogue and action and answer the question, "What is the theological or literary contribution of this aspect of the narrative?"

This is not that difficult. When I teach this material to folks with no biblical training, I am no longer surprised when they come close to discerning an OT narrative's OTM their first time around. The key is to remember to discover what each scene—in conjunction with the entire narrative—is teaching about God's nature or the way he administrates his covenants.

Analyze the Dialogue

Going scene-by-scene in the order of importance, analyze each scene's dialogue first, if it has any. This is because dialogue frequently makes a major contribution to an OT narrative's OTM.[21] Furthermore, if God speaks in a scene, look first at what he says. As the table below illustrates, it is important to recognize that God speaks in a variety of ways.

Who Speaks	Examples
God, directly	Genesis 12:1–3 (to Abraham) Numbers 20:12 (to Moses and Aaron)
God, through a dream	Genesis 28:13–15 (to Jacob) Genesis 37:6–7 (to Joseph)
God, through an intermediary	Genesis 19:12–17 (through angels) 2 Samuel 12:7–14 (through prophet)
God, through a reliable human character	Genesis 50:20 (through Joseph)

One way to make this process easier is to paste the CUT into a word-processing document, and then change the font color of God's speech to red (even if it is delivered by someone else) and all

---

21. Osborne, *The Hermeneutical Spiral*, 209; Vogt, *Interpreting the Pentateuch*, 56–57; Chisholm, *Interpreting the Historical Books*, 60–61.

other dialogue to blue. If you have a color printer, consider printing it out. Since dialogue, especially God's speech, generally makes a significant contribution to the OTM, this can be an effective visual aid. Therefore, it shouldn't come as a surprise that 12:1–14, the most important scene of its CUT, would be virtually all red.

What is the theological or literary contribution of this aspect of the narrative?	
Scene (2 Sam. 12:1–14)	Theological or Literary Contribution
¹And the Lord sent Nathan to David. . . . "There were two men in a certain city, the one rich and the other poor. ²The rich man had very many flocks and herds, ³but the poor man had nothing but one little ewe lamb. . . . ⁴Now there came a traveler to the rich man, and he was unwilling to take one of his own flock or herd to prepare for the guest who had come to him, but he took the poor man's lamb and prepared it for the man who had come to him." ⁵Then David's anger was greatly kindled against the man, and he said to Nathan, "As the Lord lives, the man who has done this deserves to die, ⁶and he shall restore the lamb fourfold, because he did this thing, and because he had no pity."	LITERARY: The dialogue in vv. 1–6 is designed to heighten interest in the story by getting David to incriminate himself leading up to God's judgment in vv. 7–14.
⁷Nathan said to David, "You are the man! Thus says the Lord, the God of Israel, 'I anointed you king over Israel, and I delivered you out of the hand of Saul. ⁸And I gave you your master's house and your master's wives into your arms and gave you the house of Israel and of Judah. And if this were too little, I would add to you as much more.	THEOLOGICAL (PRIMARY): In vv. 7–8, the Lord addresses David as king of Israel.

What is the theological or literary contribution of this aspect of the narrative?

Scene (2 Sam. 12:1–14)	Theological or Literary Contribution
⁹Why have you despised the word of the LORD, to do what is evil in his sight? You have struck down Uriah the Hittite with the sword and have taken his wife to be your wife and have killed him with the sword of the Ammonites. ¹⁰Now therefore the sword shall never depart from your house, because you have despised me and have taken the wife of Uriah the Hittite to be your wife.' ¹¹Thus says the LORD, 'Behold, I will raise up evil against you out of your own house. And I will take your wives before your eyes and give them to your neighbor, and he shall lie with your wives in the sight of this sun. ¹²For you did it secretly, but I will do this thing before all Israel and before the sun.'"	THEOLOGICAL (PRIMARY): In v. 9, the king is accused of despising the LORD's word. In v. 11, the king is punished?/disciplined?
¹³David said to Nathan, "I have sinned against the LORD." And Nathan said to David, "The LORD also has put away your sin; you shall not die. ¹⁴Nevertheless, because by this deed you have utterly scorned the LORD, the child who is born to you shall die."	THEOLOGICAL (PRIMARY): In v. 13, the king repents sincerely, God forgives king, and thus will continue to use him. In v. 14, discipline remains.

By analyzing the dialogue in 12:1–14, we discover these verses make the following contribution to its OTM:

> The LORD will forgive/not reject the kings of Israel if they sincerely repent of despising the LORD's word, but God's discipline will remain.

Analyze the Action

Once a scene's dialogue has been analyzed, it's time to analyze its action. If God acts in a scene, look first at his actions. It's important to recognize that God acts through a variety of means:

Who Acts	Examples
God, directly	Genesis 1:1 (creation) Genesis 11:8 (language confusion)
God, through biology	2 Samuel 12:15–18 (child's death) 2 Samuel 12:24 (Solomon's birth)
God, through an intermediary	Genesis 32:24–25 (Jacob's wrestling) Daniel 3:24–25 (rescue from furnace)
God, through human characters	Joshua 7:2–5 (military defeat) 2 Samuel 12:26–31 (military victory)

When we analyze a scene's action, we must be familiar with the retribution principle and the text's latest Old Covenant expansion (see Step 2), so we can discern all of God's actions. Below is an analysis of the action in 2 Samuel 12:24–25:

\multicolumn{2}{c}{What is the theological or literary contribution of this aspect of the narrative?}	
Scene (2 Samuel 12:24–25)	Theological or Literary Contribution
²⁴Then David comforted his wife, Bathsheba, and went in to her and lay with her, and she bore a son, and he called his name Solomon. And the LORD loved him ²⁵and sent a message by Nathan the prophet. So he called his name Jedidiah, because of the LORD.	THEOLOGICAL (PRIMARY): Since the birth of Solomon is a fulfillment of the next step of the Davidic Covenant and is further proof that God will use repentant kings of Israel, "fulfill the Davidic Covenant" needs to be added to the OTM.

Here is a brief theological analysis of the scenes in 2 Samuel 11–12:

	What is the theological or literary contribution of this aspect of the narrative?
Scene (vv.)	**Theological (T) or Literary (L) Contribution**
11:1–5	(L) These verses serve to exemplify what God calls despising him/his word in 12:9–10.
11:6–25	(L) These verses further exemplify what God calls despising him/his word in 12:9–10.
11:26–27	(L) These verses further exemplify what God calls despising him/his word in 12:9–10. (T-ancillary) The narrator's comment in v. 27b informs readers that God is aware of what's happened and is displeased. Kings of Israel are not allowed to use "legal" means to commit murder.
12:1–14	(L) Verses 1–6 add drama to the narrative by getting King David to incriminate himself. (T-primary) Verses 7–14 indicate that God will forgive/not reject kings of Israel—represented by David—if they sincerely repent of despising the LORD's word, but they won't escape God's discipline.
12:15–23	(L) These verses function to exemplify God's discipline as stated in 12:14.
12:24–25	(T-primary) In light of the latest Old Covenant expansion—the Davidic Covenant in 2 Samuel 7:8–16—and David's genuine repentance in 12:13, these verses indicate that God will use repentant kings of Israel to fulfill the Davidic Covenant.
12:26–31	(T-primary) In light of the retribution principle, these verses function to reinforce the idea that God will use repentant kings of Israel.

Write the Original-Theological Message

Crafting an OT narrative's OTM is tricky because we are condensing the primary message of a dynamic narrative into a static theological principle. No single sentence can perfectly capture every nuance of a narrative's primary message, but we can—and should—come close. Expect to write many drafts before forming one that is accurate, precise, and clear. Below are five guidelines.

Guideline 1: Be Accurate

First, OTMs need to be accurate. While there are multiple ways to express the same OTM, we need to keep error from seeping in. Error seeps in when concepts that are not taught in the narrative are added to the OTM. In the OTMs below, I've crossed out the inaccuracies:

	Inaccuracies in OTMs for 2 Samuel 11–12
(1)	God ~~longs to use individuals in Israel who are devoted to him and he~~ will discipline ~~those who ignore his will~~.
(2)	In spite of the king's sin and its consequences, God is ~~faithful to his covenant and~~ gracious to his people.
(3)	No matter how far deep the kings of Israel dig a hole for themselves through sin, God will forgive them ~~and be there for them~~ if they trust him.
(4)	God ~~redeems the king's mistakes~~.

There are a few problems with (1) above. First, there is nothing in 2 Samuel 11–12 that indicates that God "longs" for anything. Second, its message pertains not to "individuals in Israel," but to kings of Israel. Third, its message does not address those who are "devoted to him," or who "ignore his will," but to those sinful kings of Israel who repent. In terms of (2), the text doesn't teach that "God is faithful to his covenant"—although other narratives do. In terms of (3), the text doesn't teach the idea of God being "there for" kings. That's more of a contemporary idea. While I didn't cross it out, I am also uncomfortable with the "no matter how far deep" aspect of (3). Regarding (4), without qualifying the statement, it cannot be said that "God redeems the king's mistakes."

Guideline 2: Be Precise
Second, OTMs need to be precise. They should encapsulate the essence of the text's primary theological principle—not just part of it. They should capture the central and specific message that the narrative is designed to communicate. Accurate but imprecise OTMs *do* carry the weight of biblical authority, but they miss the specific message God designed their texts to communicate. Here are some imprecise OTMs:

Imprecise OTMs for 2 Samuel 11–12	
(A)	God is holy, righteous, and good and will discipline repentant kings of Israel for their sin.
(B)	God hates sin and cannot ignore it, but by repentance, the king's restoration is assured through God's love and grace.

While (A) and (B) are accurate—and thus they carry the weight of biblical authority—they are imprecise because they fail to mention a crucial part of the text's message: that God will use repentant kings of Israel to fulfill the Davidic Covenant.

Guideline 3: Write One Complete, Crisp, and Immediately Understandable Sentence
Third, an OTM needs to be one complete, crisp, and immediately understandable sentence. It needs to be one sentence because OTMs reflect a narrative's *primary* theological principle. It needs to be crisp and immediately understandable, so it can be successfully communicated once we've morphed it into the THT.

Crisp OTMs avoid wordiness. They contain no unnecessary words and rarely exceed twenty words. There is an easy way to know if an OTM is immediately understandable: Share it with someone else, and ask them to tell you what it means. If they immediately comprehend it, chances are you've satisfied this guideline.

Guideline 4: Avoid "and"

Fourth, avoid the word "and." Since OTMs from OT narratives communicate a single idea, it's usually a good idea to avoid using "and" because it may suggest the presence of more than one idea. This can be done by subsuming some ideas under others.

There are two times when it can be a good idea to subsume certain ideas under other ideas. The first is when an idea that *could* be stated in the OTM is an implication of another idea in the OTM. Take (A) from the "Imprecise OTMs" table. While 2 Samuel 11–12 teaches that "God is holy, righteous, and good," these are ancillary implications of the primary idea that "the LORD will use repentant kings of Israel to fulfill the Davidic Covenant, but despising the LORD's word brings discipline." Keep in mind, however, that while it makes sense to omit an implication from an OTM, there may still be a good place to mention it in the sermon.

The second time it is a good idea to subsume an idea under another idea is when an idea that *should* be in the OTM is implied by another idea that should be in the OTM. I recognize, for example, that an essential component of 2 Samuel 11–12's message is that God will forgive repentant kings of Israel. The word "forgive," however, does not appear in the OTM because it is implied by another essential concept: that God will use repentant kings of Israel.

Guideline 5: Simultaneously Determine the Question the OTM Answers

Multiple times throughout this step, I've mentioned the need to ask and answer the following question:

> **What question is this CUT designed to answer about God—his nature or covenant-keeping—to ancient Israel?**

While I've discussed how to arrive at the OTM, which is the answer to the question, I haven't spent any time on the question itself.

Of course, once you have the answer—the OTM—you should also have the question it answers. It's best, however, to determine the question at the same time you determine the answer. So then, throughout sermon preparation, seek both the question the OTM answers and the answer itself.

There are three benefits to determining the question an OTM answers. The first is that it helps us formulate accurate and precise OTMs. Many times, when I am struggling to nail an OTM, I hit the nail right on the head when I figure out the precise question the text is designed to answer.

The second benefit is that it helps us formulate clear OTMs. There have been many times when I have crafted seemingly excellent OTMs, only to discover they answer questions that are difficult to understand. This matters because the OTM becomes the THT, and a crucial way to enable listeners to follow the sermon is to raise the question it answers in the Focus and refer to it again as we preach through the text (more on the Engage and Focus in chapter 5). If the question it answers is worded in a convoluted or complex way, comprehension and memorability are decreased. Further, the Focus serves as the sermon's organizing question. It increases the sermon's relevance by making it clear to listeners what the sermon will be about.

I once opened a sermon from 2 Samuel 11–12 in John Ortberg-like fashion. I asked the congregation to turn to the person next to them and guess how many ambassadors the United States has to other nations and organizations. To maintain effectiveness, I followed it with the Focus, which meets the congregation's deep (but generally unconscious) need to know, "Where are you going with this message? What's it about? What am I supposed to get from it?"[22] After drawing a few brief connections between government ambassadors and ambassadors of Christ, I raised and restated in the Focus, "What kind of ambassador does God use to fulfill his plan of salvation?" I then said, "This morning, we are going to look at a story that answers that question."

---

22. Sunukjian, *Invitation to Biblical Preaching*, 199.

Step 5: Craft the Take-Home Truth

We now turn to the skills for determining the *wording* of the THT. The THT is the message of the sermon. It is a timeless or contemporary expression of the OTM. It takes the time-specific language of the OTM and replaces it with timeless or contemporary equivalents.[23] For OT narratives, it will generally serve as the only principle that we spend time applying. Notice below that the OTM's time-specific concepts, which are underlined, are replaced with timeless or contemporary equivalents in the THT.

> OTM: The LORD will use repentant kings of Israel to fulfill the Davidic Covenant, but despising the LORD's word brings discipline.
>
> THT: God will use us to fulfill his plan of salvation, but sin brings discipline.

All moves from the OTM to the THT must be hermeneutically sound. To preach with biblical authority, the words of our THT must be a genuine expression of their time-specific counterparts. Some hermeneutical bridges are easier to build than others. The move from "the LORD" to "God" is an easy one. "The Davidic Covenant" is one stage in God's plan of salvation, so that one's easy as well. "Despising the LORD's word," however, is more difficult. Does it represent sin in general, heinous sins, or those committed against other people? After consulting multiple commentaries, it became clear that it represents sin in general.

The most difficult bridge to build was with "repentant kings of Israel." Who are their contemporary equivalents? Christ? Believers today? No one? Christ is definitely *the* king. And, the passage reminds us of the need for Christ because it's only through his

---

23. As noted earlier, some modifications to this method would be necessary when preaching from the OT Law, but that's a discussion for another book!

atoning sacrifice that God could use sinful kings or anyone else to fulfill his plan of salvation. Christ isn't a genuine equivalent, because he isn't sinful and, therefore, has no need to repent. I concluded that "believers today" is the legitimate equivalent. Although the job description of a king of Israel—like that of an OT priest—was different than their contemporary counterparts, the essential characteristics of a king of Israel are the essential characteristics of a believer today.[24] This can be seen in 2 Samuel 11–12, where in 12:7 God refers to King David as an "anointed" king. Going to 1 Samuel 16:13 clarifies that this anointing was an anointing of the Spirit. Further, in 2 Samuel 12:7–14, all of the other essential characteristics of King David match the essential characteristics of believers today. Like King David, believers today are specially blessed by God, sinful, but contrite, and subject to discipline (2 Cor. 1:21–22; Eph. 1:3; 1 John 1:8–10; Heb. 12:5–6). All of this is ample justification for equating "repentant kings of Israel" with "us" (i.e., "believers today").

---

24. Klein, Blomberg, and Hubbard, *Introduction to Biblical Interpretation*, 349.

CHAPTER 3

A Succinct Commentary on 2 Samuel 11–12

Whenever we enhance our skills, few things are more helpful than instant feedback. Good habits take time to develop, and bad ones take time to work themselves out of our system. This chapter contains a succinct commentary on 2 Samuel 11–12, so that you can see how the theory and skills of the first two chapters come together in sermon preparation.

Introduction to 2 Samuel 10–20

The original audience of 2 Samuel was Israel in the Promised Land, possibly during the reign of Solomon or shortly thereafter. The primary concern was a secure existence in the Promised Land, especially as outlined in the Davidic Covenant.

First and Second Samuel address these concerns. They show how the original audience's historical situation is a continuation of what God has been doing through Israel since the days of Genesis. They narrate how Israel not only wanted a king, but wanted one like the other nations: one who "may judge us and go out before us and fight our battles" (1 Sam. 8:20). Samuel warns them that a king would rule them as he pleased. He'd tax them, draft them, and use their resources for personal gain (1 Sam. 8:10–18; cf. 2 Sam.

5:12–13). He warns that their dependence upon a worldly king would result in their loss: "And in that day you will cry out because of your king, whom you have chosen for yourselves, but the LORD will not answer you in that day" (1 Sam. 8:18). God responds by selecting and anointing Saul, a king according to the people's standards (9:1–2). The results are disastrous.

In his grace, God selects and anoints David, a man after his own heart, to succeed Saul (1 Sam. 16:6–7, 11–14). Eventually he's crowned king of Judah (2 Sam. 2:1–7) and Israel (5:1–16). God establishes a covenant with David, saying that he will secure a peaceful existence for Israel through the seed of David, who is not yet born. In this way, David's throne will be established forever (7:8–16).

Latest Old Covenant Expansion

The latest Old Covenant expansion is the Davidic Covenant (2 Sam. 7:8–16). While it demonstrates ties to earlier Old Covenant promises in Genesis 12 and 15, the Davidic Covenant contains new promises that pertain to the line of David. Here is an outline of the Davidic Covenant from 2 Samuel 7:8–16:

1. God chose David, born in humble conditions, to be king over Israel (7:8).
2. God has given David success thus far (7:9a).
3. God will make David's name great (7:9; cf. Gen. 12:2).
4. God will appoint a place and plant Israel there (7:10a).
    - This will be Israel's own place (7:10b; cf. Gen. 15:7).
    - Israel will not be disturbed/afflicted by enemies (7:10b–11a; cf. Gen. 12:3).
5. God will give David rest from all of his enemies (7:11b).
6. God will make David a house (7:11c).
7. God will raise a seed/child not yet born to David (7:12a).
    - God will establish the child's kingdom (7:12b).
    - The seed/child shall build a temple (7:13a).

- God will establish the throne of his kingdom forever (7:13b).
8. God will be the child's father, and he will be God's son (7:14a).
    - When he sins, God will discipline him (7:14b).
    - However, God's covenantal love won't depart from him as with Saul (7:15).
9. In this way, God will establish David's house, kingdom, and throne forever (7:16).

From Text Selection to Take-Home Truth for 2 Samuel 11–12

Step 1: Select a Complete Unit of Thought
These chapters form a CUT. There are clear beginning markers at 11:1 and 13:1, but not at 12:1 and 12:15b, where the phrase "And the LORD" suggests the end of a scene. A clear end marker is found at 12:31, but not at 11:27b. That the story's problem, David's sin, isn't resolved until 12:23 indicates that these chapters form a CUT.

Step 2: Identify the Theological and Historical Contexts
Since this CUT is an OT narrative, we can know that it is designed to answer a question about God—his nature or covenant-keeping—to ancient Israel. Thus, "the LORD," or "God," will be the grammatical subject of the OTM.

The original audience of 1–2 Samuel understands that its fate is intertwined with the actions of its king. The problem, as it knows firsthand, is that kings are often disobedient to God, the ultimate source of their security. If a king's perfect obedience is a prerequisite for security in the Promised Land, then Israel's fate is all but certain.

In 1–2 Samuel, the lives of Saul and David are contrasted intentionally. Both are sinful, but for some reason David is the kind of king God uses to fulfill his plans. Saul is not. This story brings this issue into focus. It answers the question, "What kind of sinful king of Israel will God use to fulfill the Davidic Covenant?"

Step 3: Study the Plot

While at first glance the plot seems to revolve around David, Bathsheba, and their adultery, a closer look reveals otherwise. David is named forty-one times, Uriah twenty-three, the LORD fourteen, and Bathsheba only twice. The one-month process of Uriah's murder is covered in twenty verses, God's one-hour rebuke of David via Nathan in fourteen verses, and the one-to-two-month adultery-pregnancy ordeal in two verses. The narrative's most important scene is God's rebuke of David via Nathan, which has the largest concentration of dialogue at ninety percent. The second most important scene is Uriah's murder in 11:6–25. It's fifty percent dialogue, is narrated in twenty verses, and serves to exemplify God's charges against David in 12:7–14. Interestingly, David and Bathsheba's adultery-pregnancy ordeal is narrated briefly, with only seven percent dialogue.

Step 4: Determine the Original-Theological Message

God, via Nathan, delivers the bulk of the narrative's OTM in 12:7–14 through a stream of dialogue in the narrative's most important scene. In it, he encapsulates the message of 11:1–27 as "despising" God and his word. In 12:13, David responds with genuine repentance, in contrast to Saul. God preserves David's life and forgives him, but discipline will still ensue. That God will use repentant kings of Israel to fulfill the Davidic Covenant is seen in 12:24–25, which fulfills the promise in 2 Samuel 7:12 that a seed of David's "shall come"—future tense—to rule the throne. This is fascinating because David already had six sons before the promise was made (2 Sam. 3:1–5). This turn of events probably surprised the original audience as Solomon, Israel's king, is born. Keeping the retribution principle in mind, that God will continue to use David/sinful kings of Israel who repent sincerely is confirmed further in 12:26–31, where God grants Israel a military victory (cf. 11:1).

OTM: The LORD will use repentant kings of Israel to fulfill the Davidic Covenant, but despising the LORD's word brings discipline.

THT: God will use us to fulfill his plan of salvation, but sin brings discipline.

Step 5: Craft the Take-Home Truth

The move from "the LORD" to "God" is an easy one. "The Davidic Covenant" is one stage in God's plan of salvation, so that one's easy as well. A careful look at "despising the LORD's word" indicates that this is a reference to sin in general, not just heinous sins or those committed against another person.

The move from "repentant kings of Israel" to "us" (believers today) is legitimate. Although the job description of a king of Israel (like that of an OT priest)[1] was different than that of a believer today, the essential characteristics of a king of Israel are the essential characteristics of a believer today. This can be seen in 2 Samuel 12:7, where God refers to King David as an "anointed" king. Going to 1 Samuel 16:13 clarifies that this anointing was an anointing of the Spirit. Further, in 2 Samuel 12:7–14, all of the other essential characteristics of King David match the essential characteristics of believers today. Like King David, believers today are specially blessed by God, sinful, but contrite, and subject to discipline (2 Cor. 1:21–22; Eph. 1:3; 1 John 1:8–10; Heb. 12:5–6). All of this is ample justification for equating "repentant kings of Israel" with "us"—believers today.

---

1. Klein, Blomberg, and Hubbard, *Introduction to Biblical Interpretation*, 349.

Part II:
Deliver the Message

CHAPTER 4

Initial Considerations

We've studied the CUT. We know it inside and out. We've nailed its THT. Now we're ready to put the sermon together! Before we do, let's take a step back to think through both the characteristics of excellent sermons and the most common ways OT narratives are preached. Preaching with excellence is more than the practice of useful pragmatic skills. It's purposeful communication that flows from a holistic view of preaching. It's servant-speaking, and it encourages us to develop skills that may not play to our natural strengths.

Four Pillars of Excellent Preaching

Excellent preaching is accurate, relevant, clear, and inspiring to listen to. Awareness of these pillars allows us to make informed decisions throughout the sermon creation process. They help us steer clear of lopsided choices, such as those that increase our inspirational quotient but kill our clarity. We maximize our effectiveness when we keep them in balance.

Accuracy
Excellent preaching begins with accuracy. Accurate preaching is more than biblically true—it's textually accurate. Ideally, it is also textually

precise. If the primary message of a passage is, "We should continue to follow Christ, so that we have nothing to fear when Christ returns," we should not limit our THT to "We should follow Christ." Yes, it's accurate, but it fails to proclaim the specific message of that text in favor of a general one that is taught in many passages.

Accuracy requires more than a proper understanding of a text. It requires us to communicate it with others. Comprehension does not always equal communication. I learned this back in seminary. A classmate delivered an inaccurate message, which prompted the professor to ask gently, "What was the passage about?" My classmate gave a solid response to which the professor replied, "Why didn't that get into your message?" Wide-eyed and open-mouthed, my classmate answered, "I don't know."

Accuracy extends beyond the THT to application. For application to be accurate (indeed, for it to be application at all), it must derive from the theology of the preaching text. Even if our THT is accurate, we lose accuracy when our application veers off course. If the THT is, "We should align ourselves with God's redemptive plans, because God's redemptive plans will prevail," the application must show listeners how the fact that "God wins" should motivate us to faithful living. It would be inaccurate to instead show what it would look like to "trust in God's timing when it comes to witnessing."

Relevance

Excellent preaching is also full of relevance. There are two kinds of relevance: (1) connecting the text/sermon to real life and (2) making application.

We make connections when we relate the text and its message to contemporary life. For example, when a character in a narrative faces difficulty, we can help listeners feel the struggle by describing a similar situation in today's world. This is different than making application. We make application when we show people what it looks like to put the theology of the text into practice.

It's important to remember that our job is to show the Bible's relevance, not "make it relevant." We "make" it relevant when we *use* the preaching text to prescribe things it doesn't prescribe. This tends to happen when preachers misunderstand the saying, "one interpretation, many applications," thinking it means we can freely "apply" texts in any way that seems biblical or reasonable. Instead it means that the original message can be properly applied to multiple, but limited number of, situations. We are called to uncover those situations and show listeners what bearing the message has on them.

Clarity

Excellent preaching is also clear, orally clear. An orally clear message is one in which listeners know *throughout the sermon* why we're saying what we're saying, can see for themselves what we're teaching in the text, and remember the THT for at least an hour after church.

Oral clarity is the most neglected of the four pillars. We don't think our sermons are unclear because we created them; they make sense to us. Further, listeners rarely complain about our clarity and may even blame themselves for their inability to follow our messages. When I was in college, I would go out to eat with friends after church. We would share our delight in the sermon. "Wasn't that a great message!" We all agreed, but inevitably someone would ask, "What was it about again?" Outside of some illustration or nugget of wisdom, no one ever knew, but we never thought to blame the preacher.

There are three telltale signs that our clarity can be improved. The first is the presence of detailed sermon notes in the bulletin. Good sermons are rarely enhanced by giving listeners more than one side of a half-sheet of notes. Once when I told a class that I am not a fan of detailed bulletin notes, a successful pastor protested, "My congregation demands them!" I replied, "That's because it's the only hope they have of following you." He frowned in agreement.

The second sign is the receiving of thanks for things we never said or barely touched on in the sermon. "Pastor, thank you for reminding us to put God before our careers." That was nice, but we wonder, *When did I say that?* It's a common experience for orally clear preachers to hear listeners mention the THT.

The third sign is the frequent use of cross-referencing. We justify heavy cross-referencing in a number of ways: the desire to amplify an idea, prove it's taught elsewhere in the Bible, or give listeners broader exposure to the canon. We may even feel the Bible has a somewhat magical power: The more verses people are exposed to, the more they can grow spiritually. What few of us want to admit is that cross-referencing is useful for filling time.

Cross-referencing kills oral clarity. When we depart from the preaching text, the sermon usually goes sideways. It loses focus. Eager listeners might like it, but the minds of most drift, waiting to be pulled back by some interesting comment or story. How sad to take hours to build a sermon that few can follow or remember.

Cross-referencing can also be a bit disingenuous. When we select a single passage (instead of a theme or topic) as the basis of the sermon, we have an obligation to preach that text, to focus on its unique attributes and message. Cross-referencing causes the sermon to depart from that aim, often in favor of a more generic systematic-theological treatment of a topic. Topical preaching has its place, but not when one passage is singled out as the preaching text.

Some pastors, even those at large churches with lots of amenities, have wondered how longstanding members, after being "fed" for so many years, could transition easily to a church down the street with a starkly different philosophy of ministry. What they may have never considered is the role their poor oral clarity plays. If listeners are not able to see our concepts in the text, if they can't follow our sermons, then there is a good chance they are not being "fed" as much as we suppose. What would compel them to stay if the pastor at the other church has the same problem, but does it in a more inspiring way?

Inspiring

Excellent preaching also inspires. It inspires listeners to put the message of the text into practice. Inspiring messages move the affections. They touch the heart. We can inspire without catering to people's whims or avoiding difficult topics. I was once present to hear Craig Oliver preach. In the middle of the sermon, I couldn't believe how direct he was in calling people to abandon their sin. I thought, *If I said what he is saying, people would feel discouraged and depressed, but when he says it, I feel respected and encouraged.*

It's important to distinguish between dynamic preachers and inspiring preaching. Dynamic preachers own the room. They command involuntary attention. What makes them dynamic varies. It could be their voice, wit, creativity, charisma, reputation, or sheer force of personality.

Many dynamic preachers also inspire, but not necessarily. Preachers will fail to inspire when they do not project a friendly feeling toward the audience. We fail to project a friendly feeling when we feel—despite our cognitive denials—that we are better than our audience or are a special gift of God to the world. We may take preaching too seriously (or is it not seriously enough?) by adopting a "text-centered, text-focused" approach instead of a "text-centered, audience-focused" one. Instead of envisioning ourselves as standing among the congregation and sharing God's Word, we may picture ourselves standing over the congregation and preaching at them.

The marks of an uninspiring message are subtle, but discernable. There's usually a tinge of anger in the preacher's voice. A colleague once put his young daughter to sleep to the sound of Chuck Swindoll's preaching. Naturally, it worked! When the radio station switched its programming schedule, another dynamic preacher took the bedtime slot. Within days, his daughter complained, "Daddy, can we turn that man off? He's angry." Other marks include a failure to smile, poor eye contact, chopping arm gestures, and closed fists.

The reactions to this pillar are diverse. You may feel the need to inspire is obvious, a no-brainer. You may also feel that the ability to inspire is unlearnable—you have it or you don't. But take heart! Although we may never be able to inspire like John Ortberg, Chuck Swindoll, or Craig Oliver, we can learn to do it.

I know a preacher who, early in his ministry, took preaching so seriously that he could not visualize smiling in the pulpit, much less do it. Instead of showing listeners how to put God's Word into practice, he sought to apply the text by pointing out all the ways listeners disobeyed the text. One day, a successful Lutheran pastor and friend heard him preach. After the sermon, his pastor friend said, "In so many ways your sermon was sublime, but I never want to hear you preach again." The reason? While the handling of the text was solid, the preacher's tone was too serious, his examples too negative, and he didn't appear to be delighted to be there. The preacher took those words to heart, and over the next two years developed his ability to inspire.

You may be wary of the need to inspire. It may make you feel uncomfortable. You may feel there is a close relationship between touchy-feely preachers and exegetically poor preaching (much like touchy-feely preachers often see a close relationship between exegetically astute preachers and sermons that are irrelevant or uninspiring). Or you may look at that handful of dynamic preachers who are successful in spite of their refusal to use humor or appeal to the emotions and conclude it's not necessary.

Some argue that it's unbiblical. As Paul says in 1 Corinthians 2:4–5, "My speech and my message were not in plausible words of wisdom, but in demonstration of the Spirit and of power, so that your faith might not rest in the wisdom of men but in the power of God." Paul, however, is not condemning the use of plain (or Aristotelian) rhetoric that seeks to use non-ostentatious means to enhance the effectiveness of a message. If he was, he would not have commended Apollos to the Corinthians and called him a servant of God (3:5, 9; 16:12), as Apollos was well-known for his rhetorical skills and knowledge of Scripture (Acts 18:24, 28). What Paul is addressing are the sophists and their use of overly expressive eloquence that was designed to make themselves look impressive.[1]

I embrace the need to inspire for the same reason I embrace the need to be accurate, relevant, and clear: a commitment to serve the audience. The gospel is too precious, preaching is too important, and people too valuable to give less than our best. Besides, all preaching is rhetorical—why not use rhetoric that serves others?

---

1. Thiselton, *The First Epistle to the Corinthians*, 218–23; Sunukjian, "Preacher as Persuader," 295–96.

Initial Considerations

Common Approaches to Preaching OT Narratives

Now that we've discussed the four pillars of excellent preaching, let's consider the ways preachers commonly work their way through OT narrative texts in the body of a sermon to see their potential to produce messages that are accurate, relevant, clear, and inspiring to listen to. We'll consider the merits of the verse-by-verse, alliteration, principlization, big idea, and mini-synopses approaches. Implicitly or explicitly, I will advocate for the final approach, which builds on the strengths of the first four and minimizes their weaknesses.

Verse-by-Verse

Many preachers take a verse-by-verse approach to preaching OT narratives. In this approach, the sermon is a running commentary. The preacher starts at the beginning of a passage, reads a portion of the text, makes comments or exhorts listeners, and repeats the process until the text has been covered. It's a "no-structure" approach to preaching because there is no central idea or set of key ideas around which the sermon is organized.

Pragmatically, verse-by-verse preaching can be a successful tool for stimulating church growth. It appeals to listeners who strongly desire to go to a "biblical" or "Bible-preaching" church. They may categorize preaching into two kinds—verse-by-verse and topical—and assume that verse-by-verse preaching virtually guarantees faithful proclamation of the text.

The weaknesses of verse-by-verse preaching are significant. Because the sermon has no structure, the preacher bombards listeners with an assortment of seemingly unrelated ideas. Many of these ideas are merely the preachers thoughts in response to the text, as the "applications" tend to be the result of springboarding. Furthermore, verse-by-verse preachers often preach a chapter at a time, regardless of where a CUT begins and ends; thus the sermon may be doomed before it starts.

Since verse-by-verse sermons have no unified message, listeners are unable to see how the preacher's ideas relate to each other. By the fifteen-minute mark a mental blur forms, and they are no longer able to follow the message. Preachers skilled at humor or picking fights with culture may regain listeners' attention, but listeners will have little sense of the CUT's dynamics or theology.

Alliteration

Alliteration is an approach to preaching that organizes the sermon around short phrases that begin with the same sound or letter. While other approaches may use alliteration as a device occasionally, the alliteration approach is different in that its "points" are five words or less and are rarely complete sentences.

> **Title: A Perspective on Prayer**
> I. The Purpose of Prayer.
> II. The Power of Prayer.
> III. The Perspicacity of Prayer.[2]

Alliteration is a clever but insufficient approach to preaching. It aims to create a memorable outline more than reveal the biblical text. It's rarely able to communicate a text's theology. Since its points are short phrases, not complete ideas, they usually communicate only their texts' general topics. In the preacher's mind, they represent complete ideas, but listeners—if they remember anything at all—will remember only the phrase, not its connotation. When they do express a complete idea, the use of twenty-five-cent alliterative words usually causes the text's message to be misrepresented or misunderstood.

Principlization

Probably the most commonly used approach to preaching today is principlization, which is a major cause of faux exposition. Faux exposition is non-expository preaching that results from poor

---

2. Sunukjian, *Invitation to Biblical Preaching*, 312.

attention to hermeneutics by preachers who desire to preach expository messages. We principlize when we organize the sermon around a set of principles we "see" in the text. As we discussed in chapter 1, there is usually a difference between what we "see" in the text and what the text actually teaches. It's the difference between preaching our thoughts and God's thoughts. The most obvious sign that we principlize is the presence of detailed bulletin notes with five or more "points" that are marked with a number or letter (e.g., I, II, III, A, B, C, 1, 2, 3, a, b, c, i, ii, iii).

Preachers who reject principlizing may still do it accidentally. This happens when we word contextual information or other supporting ideas in the bulletin notes in the form of principles that can be applied. Even if we avoid this trap, listeners may still see these ideas as application principles. We may know that many of the ideas on the outline aren't really "points," but listeners don't often make such distinctions.

Principlization is also a communication problem. Listeners need a small number of key ideas (at most four) on which to hang the rest of the sermon. The big picture provided by those one to four points is necessary to make sense of the rest of the sermon. For OT narratives one idea, the THT, is usually best. When we principlize, accidentally or intentionally, we give listeners too many major concepts. Once the fifth point is given, they are no longer able to process the message. By the end of the sermon, all listeners can hope to get is a feeling of encouragement and, possibly, remember some sermonic nugget.

Big Idea

Big idea preaching came to prominence with the publication of Haddon Robinson's book, *Biblical Preaching*. The book's success is a testament to its simplicity. The concept of organizing a sermon—even one with multiple main points—around a single idea is genius and is adopted in this book. Here, we call it the THT.

The biggest weakness of Robinson's big idea approach is a hermeneutical one. Robinson posits that we can arrive at the theology of a passage by summarizing its words and then replacing the summary's time-specific terms with timeless ones. As we discussed in the "Universalizing the Plot Line" section of chapter 1, this approach may work for many passages in the epistles, but often not for texts from other genres. To be fair, Robinson appears to hint that more may be required when preaching narratives, but none of his examples use a different methodology.[3]

From a communication standpoint, Robinson's approach requires further development. A good sermon does more than communicate a big idea. It enables listeners to see for themselves that the preacher's major concepts are taught in the text. It also seeks to convey the dynamics of the text. Sermons from OT narratives should convey the sense of an unfolding story. God inspired texts of various genres, and we would do well to do more than strip them down to bottom-line principles. Robinson understands these things, but leaves it to others to develop his approach further.

Mini-Synopses

Many homileticians continue Robinson's pursuit of excellent preaching. One of them is Donald Sunukjian, whose groundbreaking work in oral clarity has significantly advanced the aims of excellent preaching. Among his many contributions is a simple and elegant concept called "mini-synopses." A mini-synopsis is a summary of a biblical text that is spoken immediately prior to reading that text. He writes, "During your message, when you come to some verses that you intend to read, first give a mini-synopsis, or summary, of what the listener will learn in the reading."[4]

The simple act of telling readers what they will see in the verses about to be read does wonders for listener comprehension. Normally, preachers do one of two things. They tell listeners after reading a portion of the text what they were supposed to get out of it, or they tell listeners about the text without looking at it. Either

---

3. Robinson, *Biblical Preaching*, 41–42, 60–65.
4. Sunukjian, *Invitation to Biblical Preaching*, 294.

way, listeners don't see what we are saying in the text, and are left to take our word for it. When this happens authority resides in the preacher, not the text. Sunukjian adds that listeners' "faith is now in the words of the speaker rather than the words of Scripture."[5]

There are two kinds of mini-synopses: main points and movements. Main points are single, application-oriented sentences that encapsulate the precise theological message of their texts. They are used with passages that communicate their theology directly or briefly, such as proverbs, the sayings of Jesus, and most parts of an epistle. When a sermon has multiple main points, one of them is selected as the organizing idea of the sermon (i.e., the THT); *thus when a sermon, like those from OT narratives, have one main point, that main point is the THT.*

Movements are the second type of mini-synopses. They are descriptive, often multi-sentence, summaries of their descriptive texts. For our purposes, a descriptive text is a portion of a CUT that primarily makes a literary contribution.

Mini-synopsis movements are crucial to preaching OT narratives with excellence. They empower us to capture interest and inspire listeners without resorting to misapplication. They allow us to work our way through a text in a clear and coherent manner and to convey the story and its plot dynamics in a way listeners can see and feel for themselves. With mini-synopses, listeners "experience satisfaction in perceiving [what we say] in the reading, and they are able to visually connect the concept with the actual words in the verses."[6]

Although movements are the primary way we'll preach through the text, they're not the only way. Chapter 7 discusses other options, and chapter 8 provides guidance on when to "officially" state the THT in the body of the sermon.

---

5. Ibid., 295.
6. Ibid.

CHAPTER 5

CREATE THE INTRODUCTION

Excellent sermons have effective introductions. It's important to realize that the opening of a sermon is only one part of an introduction. Introductions contain multiple stages that work together to capture attention, open listeners' hearts, establish an urgent need to listen, and prepare listeners to hear the rest of the message.

Introductions are troublesome. If we dismiss their value or don't know how to put them together well, we can diminish the sermon's effectiveness right as it starts. Further, preparing them too early in sermon preparation may lead us to preach a disjointed sermon or to miscommunicate the text's message by changing it to fit the introduction. Waiting until later in sermon preparation is generally advised, but that may also leave little time to create an effective one or one at all.

This chapter is broken into two sections. The first discusses the major aims of an introduction. The second builds on the first and provides the steps to putting an excellent one together.

Major Aims of an Introduction

Identification
Have you ever noticed that no one is exactly like you? You have a unique personality. A unique background. A unique vision for

your church. In this fallen world, our uniqueness produces a degree of alienation among people, as Adam and Eve discovered. We get excited about things others don't care about. We show love in ways others may not appreciate. We have weaknesses others can't understand, and vice versa.

The heightened pressure of the preaching moment can deepen the alienation gap. Ordinarily, we feel safest in one-on-one conversations with people who love us and know us well. That sense of safety allows us to relax and more easily build relationships. Preaching doesn't usually feel as safe. This subtle difference in relaxation can make the mildly controlling personality appear angry. It can cause a laid-back person to appear stiff. Our nervousness, however slight or unconscious, can limit our ability to smile and cause us to stumble over words, look at our notes frequently, or avoid direct eye contact with listeners.

The first and most significant aim of an introduction is to overcome the alienation gap. This is called identification. It occurs as we reach out to listeners and form a relational bond, an interpersonal unity, based on mutual respect, shared values, and audience expectations. Through identification, listeners sense that our interests are theirs, and so open their hearts to the message we preach.

If we neglect to identify with listeners, we will fail to earn their trust. From the moment we walk to the pulpit, listeners seek to discern, "How much can I trust this person?" To the naïve preacher, this is great news: "They can trust me completely. I went to seminary. I study the Bible in Greek and Hebrew. I pull no punches. I preach straight from the Word of God."

We could argue all day about what should make a preacher appear trustworthy, but these are generally not characteristics (even godly) people look for. They don't assess our credibility based on our ability to study the Bible or preach accurately because they assume we have these skills. They also know that interpretations can vary, and since few listeners have the time, energy, resources, or inclination to become Bible experts, they are dependent upon other factors to discern our credibility.

Even pastors of large churches should not automatically assume they have gained their listeners' trust. Many people select a home church for reasons other than their love for us preachers or what they get out of the sermon. They may love the worship or enjoy being around people who are demographically similar. They may feel a connection with their small group or delight in serving in a particular ministry. They may feel the church, with its excellent children's or student ministries, provides the best opportunity for keeping their kids in the faith.

While identification can increase or decrease at any point in the sermon, it needs to be established in the introduction, preferably in the Engage, so that listeners can hear the rest of the message emotionally unencumbered. The following three questions can guide us as we seek to identify with listeners.

Is the Preacher Like Me?
Listeners trust those who are like them. Sabrina was a public-speaking student. Her final assignment was a persuasive speech. Her goal was to persuade her classmates to take their studies seriously because those without a college education tend to be paid poorly. She shared how difficult life was for her when she moved out at eighteen and joined the ranks of the employed. Earlier in the semester, I shared my own stories and told the class the same thing. Why was Sabrina far more effective than me? Because Sabrina was like them.

It's for this reason that pastors with Ph.D.'s rarely lead megachurches. It's difficult for them to identify with a wide range of listeners. They tend to have interests and concerns that most folks don't. Often their demeanor, vocabulary, or penchant for discussing obscure details communicate, "He's nice, but he's not like me."

It would be a mistake, however, to think that demographics is the deciding factor in whether listeners feel we are like them. College students who are shy, idealistic, or bombastic can easily make themselves appear quite different from their peers. Excellent preachers draw out enough similarities between them and a cross-section of listeners to make them feel alike. Indeed they must, if they wish to reach people in our increasingly multi-ethnic churches and communities.

Preachers can begin to identify with listeners by highlighting their similar values or experiences. This is what Paul did in Acts 13:16–17, 17:22–23, and 20:18–21. Watch Martin Luther King, Jr.'s "I Have a Dream" speech to see an exceptional example. The values and experiences that can unify us are many. We could highlight a broad similarity with a story about driving to church or getting that first job. Empty-nesters could begin to identify with parents of young children with a story from their own child-rearing days.

Identification is also about what not to do. We must resist the temptation to draw unnecessary distinctions between us and listeners. This is not being fake; it's servant leadership. We must grow in our understanding of how most people interpret the world and also notice how we're different than them—without feeling in the slightest that we're better than them. Those of us who didn't grow up in the church or who are highly anything (e.g., introverted, extroverted, laid back, or driven) may see the world very differently than most listeners. If we're not careful, we can say or do seemingly harmless things that will have negative and lasting effects on identification.

The key is to know your audience, be intentional, and be real. Some speakers try to fit in by mimicking the audience's accent or using the local vernacular, to their loss. In the early 2000s, I gave a presentation to a large company in Texas. My introduction included a joke about President Bush, the kind that made people of all political stripes in California laugh. But in Texas, the joke failed, and I was immediately and permanently labeled an outsider.

Does the Preacher Like Me?

Identification requires that listeners feel we like them. I would go further and suggest they need to feel we delight in them. Parents realize this early on. Our influence over our children is hindered, if they don't sense that we delight in them in spite of their missteps. This is why dynamic authoritarian preachers may have less impact on the spiritual lives of their flock than they might think—because their listeners must protect themselves by listening with their heads more than their hearts, and possibly also by redirecting the negative feelings the preacher directs their way toward other people (e.g., by judging them).

Projecting friendliness starts with the heart and grows through practice. In our hearts, we must give up any desire to exert control over listeners. We need to respect their autonomy, even as we seek to be agents of change. Attempts to use body language or words to subtly (or overtly) "make" people see their sin or live up to our personal standards will ultimately fail. Further, we must not use the pulpit to satisfy our need to feel important, influential, powerful, or worthwhile, or to adopt the persona of our favorite preacher. Using the pulpit to meet our needs is parasitic upon preaching and decreases our identification.

We must admire our listeners. This doesn't mean we admire everything about them. It means we honor the image of God in them and appreciate their courage to navigate through life. We may find this difficult. Listeners are a jumbled mess—like us! Some are even hostile toward us. Maybe you feel at times like Paul in Acts 17:16, whose "spirit was provoked" in Athens by rank idolatry. If so, notice a few verses later that Paul didn't let that keep him from finding something admirable about his listeners:

> So Paul, standing in the midst of the Areopagus, said: "Men of Athens, I perceive that in every way you are very religious. For as I passed along and observed the objects of your worship, I found also an altar with this inscription, 'To the unknown god.' What therefore you worship as unknown, this I proclaim to you" (Acts 17:22–23).

The willingness to admire the congregation is an act of humility. In the context of exhibiting church unity, Paul writes, "In humility count others more significant than yourselves" (Phil. 2:3). What better place to show it than in the pulpit? It is not surprising, then, that Augustine drew large audiences: "The secret of his [Augustine's] success is that he makes allies of his congregations, identifying himself with them and addressing them as 'we' and 'holy brethren.' He is realistic about their limitations but he never belittles them, remembering that Christ is at work among them. . . . He is both a towering theologian and a sensitive pastor."[1]

There are four skills that can increase our ability to project friendliness. A few preachers can do them well without the heart attitudes described above, but generally there is a close relationship between our heart attitude *in the pulpit* and our ability to implement these skills.

First, smile warmly. A warm smile communicates, "I love you. I care about you. I feel safe up here. You're my friend." Sunukjian sums up the research: "A preacher's facial expression is the single most important factor in whether his hearers will feel liked or not. Listeners judge from a speaker's face far more than from his words . . . as to whether he is favorably disposed toward them or not."[2]

Second, make steady eye contact with many people in the audience. It can surprise us to learn that our eye contact is moderate-to-poor. How is that possible, we rarely look at our notes? Sometimes it's because we look at our notes more often than we think, especially when delivering important parts of the sermon (e.g., the opening, movements, THT, or conclusion).

Looking at notes, however, is not the primary indication of poor eye contact. It's the location of the eyes and length of the eye contact. Many of us don't realize we tend to look over people's heads, which is a sign of fear. It's easier to be bold when we aren't looking someone in the eye. We may have also formed a habit of looking at some sections of the audience more than others. We need to look in the eyes of individuals in all sections of the room.

The length of our eye contact is also significant. We need to develop the ability to look at individuals for three to four seconds at a time. Darting from eye to eye can barely be considered eye contact.

---

1. Dunn-Wilson, *A Mirror for the Church*, 93, 98.
2. Sunukjian, "The Credibility of the Preacher," 262.

We do it because prolonged eye contact with (scary!) listeners makes us feel vulnerable. The first few times I tried to be intentional about making prolonged eye contact, my mind froze; it went blank at the two-second mark. Fortunately, it was during informal practice with a small number of people in the middle of the week!

Third, keep the chin either level or tilted slightly down. Doing this conveys a sense of equality and respect. It invites listeners to connect with us. Preaching with a raised chin projects condescension. Listeners may conclude (rightly?) that we're full of ourselves or that we think we're better than them. It can give the impression that we have already decided *for them* that what we have to say is important.

Fourth, use a friendly tone of voice. A colleague once told me a story of a former student who wanted to know how to improve in this area. He tried, but found himself unable to do it. My colleague recommended that he visualize himself preaching to his young children, presumably without resorting to a falsetto voice. That was great advice. We cherish our little kids (or grandchildren). We probably delight in them more than anyone else. We know they love us, and we fully believe in their potential. As such, we couldn't help but preach to them with a friendly voice and a heart full of joy. The thought of preaching at them with a neutral or hostile voice would be unimaginable!

The more listeners are convinced that we like them, the more their hearts open to hear the Word of God. Sunukjian writes:

> When a listener feels a speaker loves him, he is ready to accept almost anything the speaker says. When a listener says to himself, "I feel safe with this speaker; I do not doubt his motives; I do not believe he would knowingly harm me or lead me wrong; I believe he means me well; he can be trusted because of his kind intention toward me"—then that listener has given that speaker great access to his heart.[3]

---

3. Ibid.

Does the Preacher Meet My Expectations?

Part of the reason people listen to sermons is to receive pastoral counsel that's grounded in the Word of God. It's assumed that we, as vocational ministers, have professional competence—a higher level of character, training, experience, and ability that qualifies us to lead and preach. Our distinctiveness could be seen as an obstacle to identification, but it's not because listeners expect this. Our professional competence only decreases identification if we rub it in their faces (e.g., by using a sophisticated vocabulary or presenting ourselves as perfect) or appear unqualified to preach (e.g., because of inadequate speaking skills).

Meeting audience expectations is not about changing the message itself. We don't use biblical texts to preach American pragmatic ideals or the good ideas that pop into our minds in response to a text, even if that's what the audience expects. Likewise, we don't refrain from mentioning concepts like repentance or from preaching unpopular texts just because they make listeners uncomfortable. That's not identification; that's ministerial malpractice! Remember, identification exists because differences exist. We use the available means to identify with listeners in cooperation with the Holy Spirit to be a vessel through which they (and us) identify more completely with the plans and purposes of God.

Meeting our listeners' standards of professional competence requires that we become familiar with their expectations. Many standards are common to most churches and communities, but some are audience-specific. Further, some expectations may need to be met earlier in the week (e.g., pastoral visitation) or right before the church service begins (e.g., greeting people), and exceeding these expectations can increase identification.

Establish Relevance

The second major aim of an introduction is to establish the relevance of the sermon. Listeners have a natural desire to know, "What's in it for me? Why should I listen?" So then, in the Engage or Focus, we need to bring up real-life scenarios or mention areas of life that are affected by the THT.

Let's say the THT answers the question, "Why should we align ourselves with God's redemptive plans?" We could establish relevance in the Engage by opening with one or two scenarios in which people are tempted to go their own way. The first could be of an unbeliever who has ignored God's plans in order to achieve success. The second could be of a Christian who finds himself (and by extension, his family) seemingly rewarded financially for consistently working excessive hours. After providing the scenarios, we would then transition to the Focus, where we would state and restate, "When we're in situations like these, Why should we align ourselves with God's redemptive plans?" and then add something like, "This morning we're going to look at a passage that answers that question." The burning need to listen has been established, and listeners have a desire to hear the rest of the message.

There are ways to establish relevance early on, even when our Engage does not include real-life scenarios. When we restate the question in the Focus, we can mention one or two areas of life that are affected by the message of the text. For example, if the question in the Focus is "Why should we align ourselves with God's redemptive plans?" we could follow that with: "When living life apart from God seems to work for us, why should we change course and align ourselves with his redemptive plans? When, as Christian parents, our family seems to benefit from our excessive work hours, why should we entrust ourselves fully to God's redemptive plans? This morning we are going to look at a story that answers that question." It is important to note, however, that when we restate the question in the Focus in this way, the audience expects us to make application to those areas later in the sermon, so be sure to do it.

Prepare Listeners to Follow the Rest of the Sermon

The third major aim of an introduction is to prepare listeners to follow the rest of the sermon. In a review of a book of sermons by well-known preachers, I found it interesting that none of them prepared listeners in the introduction to hear the rest of the message. While I'm sure the sermons were well-received, it's doubtful that listeners were able to follow them. Excellent preparation and penetrating insight can be totally lost when listeners leave the introduction with no idea what the sermon is about or the direction it's going to take.

The most obvious way, when preaching from OT narratives, to prepare listeners to follow the rest of the message has already been discussed: stating and immediately restating the question the THT answers in the Focus and adding a line like, "This morning we're going to look at a passage that answers that question." Some homileticians bristle at such obvious sign-posting, feeling it draws too much attention to the inner workings of the sermon, but make no mistake, listeners disagree. They love it when we make it clear to them what the sermon is about.

Still, we shouldn't rely exclusively on the Focus to prepare listeners for the rest of the sermon. Like the sermon as a whole, the entire introduction should be designed to make it easy for listeners to follow us, as the next section discusses in greater detail.

Stages of an Introduction

Introductions consist of up to five stages in this order: Engage, Focus, Set the Stage, Preview, and Announce the Passage. It's not always necessary to Set the Stage or to Preview, but the other stages are virtually always necessary. It's important to maintain the order of the stages because it represents the natural way humans prepare to hear a message. It also minimizes the chances that listeners will become distracted in the opening minutes. For example, if we Announce the Passage before we Set the Stage, listeners will be distracted as they turn to the text, unable to pay close attention, as we share the crucial background information they need to understand the rest of the message.

Engage and Focus

The first two stages, Engage and Focus, are so connected we'll discuss them together. The Engage is the sermon opening. The goal here is to identify with the audience and gain involuntary attention that leads seamlessly to the Focus.

The Focus will either contain the THT (deductive) or *preferably, the question it answers* (inductive). Going inductive is almost always the better choice, because it adds tension and interest to the sermon. It invites listeners to join us on a quest to discover the answer to the question. Unless the THT is so gripping or controversial that it captivates listeners, going deductive will reduce interest in the sermon. How could it not? We spill the beans up front. It shouldn't surprise us, then, that a recent study found that listeners of all generations prefer sermons with an inductive Focus.[4]

The Engage should gain "involuntary attention." Involuntary attention is achieved when listeners pay attention because they are compelled to. Their hearts are captivated, eager and open to hear what comes next. Securing involuntary attention is a service to listeners because it makes listening effortless. It reduces the mental and physical energy needed to listen and makes listening a pleasant experience. Preachers, however, normally settle for "voluntary attention"—the polite kind of attention that listeners give us because they're at church.

Knowing how to gain involuntary attention helps us make excellent choices in the Engage. What gains involuntary attention?

- Movement, such as when the preacher walks out from behind the pulpit.
- Activity, such as when listeners are brought on stage to do something.
- Interaction, such as getting the audience to talk to the person next to them.
- Extremes, such as showing/picturing something bright or large.
- Suspense or conflict, such as picturing difficult real-life situations the sermon will address.

---

4. Featherstone, "Evaluating the Effectiveness of Five Forms of Expositional Preaching," 11.

- The existential, such as topics like life, death, success, health, and happiness.[5]

A word of caution: Be creative, but don't go over-the-top; it's counterproductive. While extravagant openings and outright showmanship gain involuntary attention and may increase attendance, it will also cause listeners to take you and the message less seriously. A little creativity goes a long way. Gaining involuntary attention through "ordinary" means is effective. We listen to those who serve us; we are entertained by those who wow us.

Brief Story or Illustration

One way to begin a sermon is with a brief story or illustration that creates interest in and leads directly to the Focus. What makes this difficult is the need to move seamlessly from the Engage to the Focus. Although it can be easy to find a compelling story that relates generally to the topic at hand, it can be difficult to come up with one that leads directly to the Focus.

For example, if the Focus is, "What does God call us (the local church body) to do in times of persecution?" it would confuse listeners to open with a story about how one individual faced persecution, since the sermon is about how the church as a whole should respond when it's persecuted. It would be better to Engage with a story about a church that struggled with infighting as a result of persecution. "But Ben, what if I can't find such a story?" Then use one of the other ways to open the sermon.

The other way to use a story or illustration is to raise interest in the sermon's general topic, so long as we make a seamless transition to the Focus. If the question in the Focus is, "Why should we align ourselves with God's redemptive plans?" we could open with an illustration about the desire to make a name for ourselves, *but we would need to insert a transition that ties that illustration directly to the Focus.*

---

5. Adapted from Monroe, Ehninger, and Gronbeck, *Principles and Types of Speech Communication*, 131–35.

Create the Introduction

Without it, listeners will sense in the introduction a disjointedness to the sermon. Notice how helpful such a transition can be:

> [ENGAGE] Nikita Khrushchev was president of the Soviet Union after Stalin. Khrushchev once asked a child, "Who is your father?"
>
> The boy replied, "Nikita Khrushchev is my father."
> "And who is your mother?"
> "The Communist Party."
> "Very good. Now tell me, what would you like to be when you grow up?"
> The boy replied [with a broken voice], "I wanna be an orphan."
>
> Like that boy, we all have a vision of who we want to be. We all want to be known for something. To make a name for ourselves. That vision, that name, may have changed over time. Life throws us curve balls, and we have to adapt.
>
> [transition to Focus] Let's be real. God seems to let us get away with a lot. He may discipline us, but we often don't recognize it for what it is. He calls us to align ourselves with his redemptive plans, but at a practical level we may wonder, "Why? What's the big deal?"
>
> [FOCUS] So then, why should we align ourselves with God's redemptive plans? [restate:] What's the problem with making a name for ourselves, in defiance of God's plans? This morning we're going to look at a passage that answers that question.

First Half of a Picture-Painting Application

Chapter 10 discusses how to create Picture-Painting Applications

(PPAs), concrete applications that place listeners in real-life scenarios and then show them how the THT can be lived out in those situations. An effective way to open the sermon is to put the first half of one or more PPAs in the Engage. Later, in the application section, we would call back these situations to complete the PPA by showing listeners how to put the THT into practice in them.

These scenarios must themselves flow seamlessly to the Focus. We can't use them to raise the sermon's general topic and then use transitions to tie the scenarios directly to the Focus. The scenarios themselves must lead directly to the Focus, and the THT must have some direct bearing on how to respond to them.

For example, if the Focus is "What kind of person will God use to fulfill his plan of salvation?" and the THT is "God will use us (believers who repent) to fulfill his plan of salvation, but sin brings discipline," the sermon would be disjointed and later contain misapplication if the Engage centered on a scenario in which a teenager doubts that God will use him to fulfill his plan of salvation because his friends think the gospel is silly. Instead the teenager would need to doubt God could use him because of his struggle with sin.

> [ENGAGE] One of my favorite things to do each week is to greet so many of you on your way in. I love to see your smiles. I am blessed to hear your stories, your triumphs and trials, and to pray with you. Our church is full of real people on real journeys. Each journey is different.
>
> [first scenario, existing situation PPA] Maybe you grew up in the church. You had some fun times going to children's church, Sunday school, summer camp. But somewhere along the way, you drifted. You may not have abandoned the faith, but you drifted. Possibly farther than you once thought possible. For whatever reason you're back. And "Amen" to that! Maybe you've been back for a year or a few months, maybe

weeks. Maybe today is your first time back in a while. You look at your life and wonder, "I've drifted so far for so long. Could God ever use me?"

[second scenario, existing situation PPA] Some of us are at a different place in our journey. Maybe you've been following Christ faithfully for years. You attend weekly. You're part of a small group. And yet, there is that one problem you can't seem to get a hold of. Maybe it's anger. It's hard for you to not lash out at that one co-worker or family member. You wonder, "Will God still use me?"

[third scenario, existing situation PPA] Maybe you've always maintained an excellent witness, but recently you succumbed to temptation. You got drunk at the company party. Now, everyone at work loves to joke about the afternoon the "church girl" went a little crazy. You play it off, but you're embarrassed. You feel like a hypocrite. You wonder, "Will God still use me to reach my co-workers for Christ?"

[FOCUS] That's what we are going to look at this morning—the question, "What kind of person will God use to fulfill his plan of salvation? [restate:] When God looks around the church for people to use, who will God use to further the gospel? [restate:] To what extent, if at all, can God use an imperfect believer like me to fulfill his plan of salvation?"

Explore an Intriguing Issue

Human beings crave resolution. We want to have a coherent worldview, one that can account neatly for what we think we know about the world. We do our best to label, classify, and systematize. When that seems impossible, we may compartmentalize ("tie-it-off"), fret endlessly, or catastrophize. People catastrophize when they leave the faith because they are unable to reconcile a naïve view of the faith with their current understanding of the world.

When our passage provides us with the opportunity to legitimately address an intriguing issue—one that is difficult for people to account for neatly—we do well to explore it in the Engage, and address it further as the sermon progresses. Enabling listeners to resolve a biblical or theological difficulty can break their spiritual arrested development. Various OT narratives provide opportunities to legitimately explore some, but not all, intriguing questions about God's character and providence, science and faith, and ancient, modern, and biblical ethics (e.g., war, justice, and church-state relations).

We must not, however, feed listeners false harmonizations, or demonize others or their views. Doing so may satisfy the already-convinced and the close-minded, but would likely (and needlessly) disenfranchise critically engaged young adults or other informed listeners. We must be thoughtfully conversant on the issues we discuss, make it clear when a solution is "tentative" or "possible," and not try to pass off a weak solution as plausible. When necessary, say something like, "I don't know"—which encourages listeners to relax and be okay with the unresolved "faith-life" tension.

> [ENGAGE] One of the things that distinguishes Evangelicals—that's us—from Catholics is the authority of tradition. The Catholic view is that the Church and its tradition are the final authority on many theological matters.[6]
>
> Evangelicals take a different perspective. We value tradition, but if we discover the Bible contradicts a

---

6. "Through Tradition, the Church, in her doctrine, life and worship, perpetuates and transmits to every generation all that she herself is, all that she believes." *Catechism of the Catholic Church*, 25.

view we've traditionally held to, we let go of that tradition. The Bible is our final authority. If a conflict exists between what we believe and what the Bible teaches, we side with the Bible.

Our commitment to biblical authority comes with responsibility. The Bible can only be our final authority if we're willing to read it carefully, in context. We won't always get it right, but we need to at least try.

Holding to biblical authority is courageous. Those who hold to biblical authority may wish that everyone goes to heaven, but they don't hold that position because the Bible doesn't teach it.

[transition to Focus] That brings us to one of the most important theological questions for parents today: What does Genesis 1 teach?

Why is it so important to parents? Because our kids leave the faith over it. Growing up, church kids are often taught that Genesis 1 teaches the earth is thousands of years old. That's the tradition they grew up with. It might be right; it might be wrong. What we do know is that when many kids learn that good scientific evidence indicates the earth and universe are billions of years old, they have a crisis of faith.

If Genesis 1 teaches a young earth, we need to have courage and hold to it. The Bible is the Bible. If a careful reading of Genesis 1 indicates it doesn't teach a young earth, we must be even more courageous. We must tell our children we got it wrong.

> We must hold to biblical authority, and let go of that tradition—even if we've spent thirty years traveling the country teaching young-earth creationist seminars and our income depends on it.
>
> [FOCUS] So then, What does Genesis 1 teach?[7] [restate:] Does it teach a young earth, an old earth, or something else? [restate:] What does God want us to know from Genesis 1? This morning, we are going to answer that question.

Refer to a Recent Event

On occasion, or as the need arises, the Engage should mention important events related to the community, technology, celebrity culture, or the world. Listeners have a need to know that we are in touch with what's going on in the world. When we do, it's best to stick to the facts and avoid political commentary, controversial comments, or speculation about the spiritual causes of events. So then, it would make sense to mention the previous week's general election in the Engage—so long as we can make a seamless transition to the Focus—but the pulpit is not the place to express our excitement or disappointment with the results.

> [ENGAGE] The world can be an unstable place. At the beginning of 2003, Saddam Hussein ruled Iraq. A few months later, his regime was toppled. A new government emerged. That instability in Iraq led to the persecution of Christians. There were 1.4 million Christians in Iraq before Saddam's ouster. Today, there are 400,000.

---

7. For obvious reasons, this is one of those rare occasions where it would be necessary to provide the passage reference in the Focus, instead of waiting until the end of the introduction.

> The instability in Iraq continues. We've learned recently that ISIS, a group of Islamic insurgents, has taken over parts of Iraq. They've declared Iraq a strict Islamic state and themselves as its rulers. In the parts of Iraq that ISIS controls, Christians face even greater instability. In the city of Mosul, for example, Christians have three options: convert to Islam, pay protection money, or face the sword.
>
> Things are more stable in the United States. No overthrow of the government seems likely in the foreseeable future. Yet, we can't assume that'll always be the case. World history is full of revolutions and coups. Who would have thought the good people of Germany would fall for a savage like Hitler?
>
> That brings us to the question:
>
> [FOCUS] "Why should we put our confidence in God, when some destabilizing force, some leader, group, whatever, could turn this country upside down? [restate:] Why trust God, when a perfect storm of events could turn my fortunes around, [snap fingers] like that? This morning we're going to look at a passage that answers that question.

Involve the Listeners

An excellent option for gaining involuntary attention is to involve the listeners. While it's often effective to bring a few of them onto the platform for an activity, my favorite way—which I learned from John Ortberg—is to open with an interesting question that no one would be expected to know the answer to, and then have listeners share their answers with the person next to them. Once they are done sharing, don't have them raise their hands to share their answers; there are too many risks involved.

Instead, just share your answer and transition from the question to the Focus.

> [ENGAGE] A few years ago, a friend of mine became a Foreign Service Officer. Foreign Service Officers work at American embassies all over the world.
>
> The head of each embassy is called an ambassador. Ambassadors are the highest-ranking representatives of their government in the countries they serve in. Ambassadors are granted the authority to speak in that country on behalf of the President, and by extension, the American people.
>
> In a moment, turn to the person next to you. Take a guess as to how many ambassadors the US has to foreign countries right now. Here are some clues: there are approximately 180 countries. We don't have ambassadors for some countries, like North Korea. Small countries may share an ambassador. Some ambassador positions are vacant. Okay, turn to the person next to you.
>
> [watch and smile comfortably for about a minute as listeners chat among themselves]
>
> Here's the answer: Right now, the US has 128 ambassadors to other countries. [Add a comment or two, based on the audience's reaction.]
>
> [transition to Focus] In God's kingdom, in God's eyes, every person who places their faith in Jesus Christ is an ambassador, an ambassador of Jesus Christ. That's true whether we're seven or 107. It's true whether our marriage is great, we're recently divorced, or single.

> Ambassadors of Jesus Christ are called to further God's plan of salvation. God's plan began in Genesis 3:15. It continued through Abraham. Israel. It continues through to Christ and the Gospel today, and into eternity. God calls us as ambassadors to act and speak in ways that bring people into a relationship with Jesus.
>
> We want to be a part of what God is doing. We want God to use us to further his plan. We know that God wants to use us. When we look at our lives, we also know we struggle to follow God. We make mistakes. We get sidetracked by our own plans. We sin. We wonder less, "Does God *want* to use me?" and more, "*Will* God use me?"
>
> [FOCUS] What kind of ambassador of Christ will God use to fulfill his plan of salvation? [restate:] Who among us does God use to further the gospel? This morning we're going to look at a time in King David's life that answers that question.

How Not to Open a Sermon

There are other ways to open a sermon, including those that use some combination of the above. Most any way that accomplishes identification and moves seamlessly to the Focus will be effective. However, two ways are not effective.

The first is to omit the Engage, Focus, or both. Too much rides on them to leave them out. True, listeners don't complain when we open the sermon by simply stating the preaching text, and then begin to explain it or provide background information. Nonetheless, when we do that, we miss a crucial opportunity to open wide their hearts and preach a unified sermon.

The second is to open with a "Yes/No" or "How many of you" question, unless everyone will agree and laugh as a result. For example, it can work to open with, "Raise your hand. How many of us have ever been judged by someone else?" It's funny. It gets a good laugh and relaxes the audience.

Normally, however, these kinds of questions subtly alienate a number of people. Questions like "Have you ever wondered how valuable you are in God's sight?" or "How many of you watched the World Series last week?" decrease identification because the answer is "no" for more people than we realize; many people don't ask themselves deep, reflective questions or watch the World Series. Opening this way won't ruin a sermon, but it does produce a mild emotional distance in some just seconds into the sermon, which makes it that much harder for the affected listeners to connect with us and the message.

I know how tempting it can be to start a sermon this way. I used to do it, and a quarter of my preaching students do it in their first sermon—despite multiple reminders not to! It can be hard to find a way to move seamlessly from the Engage to the Focus, and opening with questions like these can seem like an easy solution. Unfortunately, they typically hinder identification.

Fortunately, there is a simple solution, although it's not necessarily the best way to open: Convert the question into a statement. For example, "How many of you watched the World Series last week?" can become, "Last week I watched the World Series." "Have you ever wondered how valuable you are in God's sight?" can become, "It can be a wonderful thing to think about our value in Christ."

Set the Stage

After the Focus, we have the option to "Set the Stage" by providing background information that listeners will need to understand the rest of the message. It's optional, because such information is not always necessary. Many times, however, it is a good idea to Set the Stage. The key is to only include information that's (1) not mentioned in text, but (2) necessary to understand the text or its message.

For example, we wouldn't want to mention David's adultery, Uriah's murder, or Solomon's birth at this point in a sermon from 2

Samuel 11–12, because a discussion of those events will arise naturally as we preach through the CUT. Nor would it be helpful to discuss information about the book's author or original composition date because listeners don't need this information to understand the text or its message. This stage generally takes no more than one minute. If we frequently take longer, we're probably hindering the message by including unnecessary information.

What kind of information could we include? The first kind is hermeneutical context. For example, it can be useful to mention briefly that [OT narratives are designed primarily to teach us something about God.] What we don't want to do is go into a deep discussion on the matter or explain that those who take a different approach are wrong. The sermon is not the place for these kinds of discussions, and most listeners would be turned off by our self-righteousness.

It can be helpful, for example, to mention the hermeneutical connection between us and a character who is theologically representative in the THT. In my sermon from 2 Samuel 11–12, I Set the Stage by drawing connections between us and King David. I explain that, as king, he can rightly be considered an ambassador. This enables listeners to understand that God's treatment of David in this passage—and by implication not Bathsheba, Uriah, or Joab—is *broadly* paradigmatic for believers today.

The second kind of information we could include is back story. It can be helpful to mention events from earlier in the biblical book or biblical history that are vital to understanding the preaching text or its message. In my sermon from Genesis 11:1–9, I tell listeners that God, as part of his redemptive plans, called on the people to disperse. That way listeners comprehend immediately, and with joy, the significance of the people settling in Shinar, and there is no confusion about why God disperses them later.

> [SET THE STAGE] When David was alive, God had one primary ambassador: the king of Israel. The king was the primary instrument through which

> God fulfilled his purposes. Israel knew this and had a desire to know what kind of king, what kind of ambassador, God would use.
>
> David was Israel's second king. Israel's first king was Saul. Saul was an ambassador too, but God stopped using Saul after he sinned—for what we might consider lesser crimes than those we'll soon discover David commits.

Preview and Announce the Passage

We've opened with the Engage, which led seamlessly to the Focus. If helpful, we've Set the Stage. It's now time to Preview and Announce the Passage. These two stages let listeners know how we are going to get from here to the THT. They often meet in the same sentence, where the end of the Preview begins the sentence and the Announce the Passage finishes it. Since our sermons from OT narratives center on one question (the Focus), our Preview can often be as simple as raising that question again and indicating that we will find the answer (the THT) in the preaching text.

There is an art to the Announce the Passage stage. We need to do it in a way that connects to what came before, does not sound formulaic, and gets listeners to open to the CUT. Therefore, begin by mentioning only the biblical book: "To find the answer to that question, let's open our Bibles to the book of 2 Samuel." Consider putting your Bible in your hand at this point and standing comfortably away from the pulpit with a warm smile.

Next, let listeners know the approximate location of the book in the Bible: "It's in the Old Testament, between Joshua and Kings." If the church puts Bibles in the pews or under the chairs, provide the page number also: "It's on page 258 in the Blue Bibles." This may seem unnecessary, but consider the following story: I preached a sermon series once from selected texts in Genesis through Deuteronomy for a church. For the CUTs in

Genesis, I did not identify the book's general location. For the first sermon in Exodus, I thought about it, but decided against it (I didn't want to insult them!). Ironically, when I arrived the following Sunday, an elder took me aside and said, "Now that you're deeper into the Bible, it would help if you would give people a clearer idea of where the passage you're preaching from is at in the Bible."

Continue by sharing the biblical book again, this time with the chapter number: "2 Samuel chapter 11." Finally, wait a few seconds, and state the book and chapter again in short form: "2 Samuel 11." *Don't give the verse reference yet; wait until just before the first set of verses are read in the body of the sermon.* Expect this stage to take about twenty-five seconds.

> [PREVIEW] It's in the context of David's first failure as king that we discover, What kind of ambassador, indeed ambassadors of Christ today, God will use to fulfill his plan of salvation.
>
> [ANNOUNCE THE PASSAGE] To get the answer to that question, let's open our Bibles to the book of 2 Samuel.... It's in the Old Testament, between Joshua and Kings... page 258 in the Blue Bibles... 2 Samuel chapter 11... 2 Samuel 11.

As prescriptive as those recommendations are, following them proves to be quite helpful. First, it gives listeners the opportunity to find the preaching text efficiently. Yes, putting the passage reference in the bulletin can help, but a good number of people don't look at their bulletins closely. Second, it gives listeners who need help identifying the general location of a book the assistance they need. Third, it's a gentle way to help resistant listeners realize, "Oh, he really expects us to open our Bibles!" It also gives these folks an opportunity to find the passage before we move on. Fourth, it generally keeps listeners from reading ahead because the verse reference hasn't been stated yet. Fifth, it sounds natural because it's courteous to allow listeners to find the passage by providing its location in manageable chunks.

Once we've worked our way through the introduction, it's time to preach through the CUT.

CHAPTER 6

PREACH THROUGH THE CUT (PART 1): MOVEMENTS

The first concern upon entering the body of the sermon is to preach through the text. Unfortunately, preachers too often give their main points or explain their texts without pointing listeners back to the text, which keeps listeners from seeing for themselves that what we're saying arises from the text.

One result is that we accidentally treat our main points and explanations as if they are more important than the inspired Word itself. When we preach through the text, listeners shouldn't feel like we're talking about the text or retelling its story, as much as sense that they can see and feel the text and its dynamics for themselves.

We discussed in chapter 4 why the best way to preach through OT narratives is with mini-synopses, particularly mini-synopsis movements. In this chapter, we will discuss how to craft them skillfully. We will usually preach through the text by providing a movement, reading the verses it's created for, providing another movement and reading its verses, and so forth, until we've preached through the CUT.

Before we provide a movement, it is often helpful to include a transition to heighten interest in the narrative, to allude to the Focus, or to foreshadow the THT. On occasion, it may also be helpful to explain a movement's text in a little more detail after reading it. Here is an outline of the usual way we preach through the text:

- Make a transition (optional).
- Provide a movement for the verses that are about to be read.
  → Read only the verses the movement was crafted for.
  → Explain the verses just read (usually omitted).

- Make a transition (optional).
- Provide a movement for the verses that are about to be read.
  → Read only the verses the movement was crafted for.
  → Explain the verses just read (usually omitted).

There are exceptions to the basic flow above, and the following chapter discusses them. Chapter 8 then discusses where to officially state the THT. Chapters 9–12 explain what to do after we've preached through the text.

Selecting Verses for Movements

Sermons from OT narratives, especially those from multi-chapter CUTs, could have ten or more movements. The reason it's okay to have ten movements, but not ten main points, is that movements are descriptive summaries of their verses. We use them to reveal the narrative's plot dynamics. In contrast, main points are prescriptive, application-oriented statements. Movements progress a story; main points provide abstract ideas that require significant mental effort to process.

Movements take skill to craft well. Effective movements do more than summarize the verses that are about to be read—they illuminate them. Before we can create each movement, however, we need to select which set of verses go with each one.

Two guidelines affect which set of verses go with a movement. First, a movement should illuminate no more than five verses. No matter how well we craft our movements, listeners will find it difficult to "see" what we're saying in the text when we cover more than five verses of OT narrative.

Second, a movement should illuminate verses in the same scene and plot stage. This is because each scene and plot stage has its own dynamics. For example, it's not uncommon for the problem stage to end with a sense of despair and the solution stage to bring a glimmer of hope. Therefore, instead of using one movement to try to convey both dynamics, it would be better to accentuate those differences by creating a movement for each.

You might be wondering, "What if a CUT contains something like sixty verses? Do we create twelve movements or more?" The answer is no, for two reasons. First, you'll want to summarize some verses without reading them to ensure you're preaching through the CUT at a steady clip. Second, if you were to create a movement for all sixty verses, it would probably take you thirty minutes just to preach through the CUT, which is generally inadvisable.

Crafting Excellent Movements

Effective movements illuminate the text. They convey the sense that an exciting plot is unfolding. Movements are effective when they are crafted well and build on each other, with the help of transitions. *Note: All of these guidelines apply also to the alternatives to movements that are discussed in the next chapter.*

Guideline 1: Don't Word Movements Like Main Points

Principlization of OT narratives can be a hard habit to break. When some preachers first learn to create movements, the concept is so foreign to them that their initial attempts are worded like main points. Instead of providing an illuminating summary of a set of verses, they find ways to write movements as main point-like principles: "We should view the battles in our lives from God's perspective," or "Fighting for God to be known throughout the world is a cause worth fighting for." However, movements are descriptive in nature and usually multiple sentences in length.

Guideline 2: Keep the Sermon Squarely on the Focus/THT
One of the challenges of preaching OT narratives is that listeners can easily forget the question in the Focus, unless we bring it up *repeatedly* as we preach through the text. Listeners will not experience the sense of "Aha! Yes. I saw the THT in the text!" unless we allude to it whenever the text provides the opportunity.

The seriousness of this problem was reinforced recently as I was listening to a sermon by a skilled preacher at a conference. Not only did the sermon have no Focus, the THT was never alluded to. After the text was preached, listeners were clueless when the preacher raised the question, "What's the big idea of the narrative?" When he provided the answer, all we could say to ourselves was, "Huh? Okay, I'll take your word for it."

The solution to this problem is simple: Frequently incorporate language from the Focus or THT into our movements or transitions to movements as we preach through the text. Notice the italicized words in the following example:

> [MOVEMENT] And then God surprises us. God goes beyond implying that he will use his *ambassador*, King David, to further his *plans*. He proves it. Solomon is born, the one who *fulfills* the next step in God's plans. They, like us, can have confidence that *God will indeed use a sinful, sometimes wayward, ambassador like King David to fulfill his plans.*
>
> [READ] Look with me at verses 24 and 25, "Then David comforted his wife, Bathsheba, and went in to her and lay with her, and she bore a son, and he called his name Solomon. And the Lord loved him and sent a message by Nathan the prophet. So he called his name Jedidiah, because of the Lord."

Guideline 3: Put the Fruit of Sermon Preparation into Them
Sermon preparation invigorates our preaching. Although much of

what we learn never makes it into the sermon, some of it certainly should. When we strategically incorporate the fruit of our study into our movements, we help the audience experience the richness and emotion of the plot when their verses are read. It also allows us to preach through the CUT at a steady clip, because it generally makes it unnecessary for us to stop after the text has been read to explain the text in greater detail.

Skimpy movements—those that fail to provide exegetical insight into the text—commonly cause preachers to explain the text after its been read, resulting in a stop-and-go effect. That's not to say that creating robust movements will completely eliminate the need to go back to explain verses that were just read—only that it needn't happen more than a few times in a sermon, and that when it does happen, it should be brief.

What kind of exegetical fruit should we include? Any insight listeners will be able to "see" in the text after we mention it.

> [Transition] With Bathsheba pregnant, our *ambassador*-king finds himself in an unexpected predicament. How can he possibly get out of it?
>
> [MOVEMENT] Our worst fears are realized: King David resolves to murder Uriah through "legal means." His first strategy: entrapment. David calls Uriah back from battle. He hobnobs about the war. "Hey, Uriah, go enjoy some alone time with Bathsheba." Marital relations are strictly forbidden in wartime. If Uriah complies, he's liable to receive a death sentence. Uriah leaves, and David's plan looks successful, until we learn of Uriah's integrity. He sleeps not with his wife, but in the servants' quarters.
>
> [READ] Look at verses 6 through 9: "So David sent word to Joab, 'Send me Uriah the Hittite.' And

> Joab sent Uriah to David. When Uriah came to him, David asked how Joab was doing and how the people were doing and how the war was going. Then David said to Uriah, 'Go down to your house and—[coughing sound]—wash your feet.' And Uriah went out of the king's house, and there followed him a present from the king. But Uriah slept at the door of the king's house with all the servants of his lord and did not go down to his house."

Guideline 4: Make Connections to Real Life

We discussed the two types of relevance in chapter 4: drawing connections to real life and application. Application is almost never appropriate as we preach through an OT narrative, but drawing connections is vital. When the text gives us the opportunity, our movements should illuminate it by interacting at a human level with the events in the narrative or use analogies or metaphors to make connections to real life.

> [MOVEMENT] It's hard to capture the enthusiasm of Adam's response. It's something like [wide-eyed, jaw dropping], "Whoa! Wow! A companion! Someone like me! Only. . . . [cutely rolling the eyes] better! [with a deeper, slower, and slightly comical voice] A . . . lot . . . better. If we could hear the synapses of Adam's brain set to music, we'd probably hear [*Happy Days* theme song plays for ten seconds]. . . . Adam says, "Now that's a woo-mannn!"
>
> [READ] Read with me verse 23, "Then the man said, 'This at last is bone of my bones and flesh of my flesh; she shall be called Woman, because she was taken out of Man.'"

Guideline 5: Write/Speak for the Ear

This guideline applies to the entire sermon, but it seems best to discuss it here. Excellent sermons are written to be heard not read. They needn't be beautiful literary artifices or dense compositions. Sermons need to be crafted with the full realization that listeners cannot stop, reverse, and re-listen to us in the middle of the sermon. They must be able to understand what we say when we say it. We should never underestimate our ability to be unclear.

Although Robert Jacks' *Just Say the Word!: Writing for the Ear* deserves careful study, the following five tips can significantly enhance the listenability of an otherwise clear sermon. I've found that if preachers put these five tips into practice, they will automatically put many of Jacks' recommendations into practice.

Tips #1 and 2: Use Spoken Grammar and Short Sentences

Spoken grammar and short sentences are probably the two most important ways to enhance our word choice. Spoken grammar reflects the syntax and style of ordinary conversation. For example, sentence fragments are okay. No, really. Contractions *aren't* forbidden, and sentences can end with prepositions (e.g., in, at, on, to), even when they don't have to.

Spoken grammar is less formal, but it is not sloppy grammar. In most contexts, however, it is counterproductive to use "big" words out of context, double negatives, or slang.

Shorter sentences virtually force us to use the active voice. They are easier to comprehend and less stressful to listen to, because the audience isn't required to remember the beginning of a long sentence as they're listening to the rest of the sentence. Screenwriters know this. When we turn on a movie's subtitles, we can see that characters rarely use long sentences, and when they do, it's often to convey a character's incoherent or chaotic response to the situation they're facing.

Tip #3: Incorporate Dialogue

Dialogue is an effective means of (re-)engaging listeners; it increases their interest and activates their imagination. Dialogue is useful for illuminating verses with and without dialogue. When using dialogue, it's important to not merely repeat the words of the text—unless there is a compelling reason. Instead, rephrase them or expand on them to bring out the sense, to make the narrative feel a little more contemporary, and to help listeners feel the narrative's power.

> [MOVEMENT] Life gets better. God puts Adam in the Garden of Eden to enjoy restful work. That's right! The restful work of tending the Garden. As for rules and regulations, there's only one. Imagine that! God walks Adam around. "Adam, isn't this place great? Enjoy it. You can eat from any tree, *but* don't eat from this one. It's the tree of the knowledge of good and evil. You eat it . . . [finger across the throat]."
>
> [READ] Read with me verses 15–17, "The LORD God took the man and put him in the Garden of Eden to work it and keep it. And the LORD God commanded the man, saying, 'You may surely eat of every tree of the garden, but of the tree of the knowledge of good and evil you shall not eat, for in the day that you eat of it you shall surely die.'"

Tip #4: Cut Down on the Pronouns

Pronouns are words that take the place of proper or common nouns. We use them in place of names or objects to avoid sounding redundant. Pronouns are helpful as long as it's clear who or what the pronoun refers to. When it's not clear, confusion surfaces. For example, it's unclear what "it" refers to in the following sentence: "When the bicycle hit the tree, it was not damaged."

We need to cut down a bit on our pronoun use in preaching, because the dynamics of oral communication can make it difficult for listeners to discern a pronoun's referent. If for one moment a listener doesn't hear us correctly or contemplates something we just said, and that is the one time we refer to a person we're discussing by name, the next minute or two will be a frustrating experience.

The worry over redundancy is in the preacher's mind only. Audiences don't see it as being redundant. All they know is that they could follow the sermon. Therefore, don't be afraid to use proper names like "David" in two straight sentences. When describing a scene with two characters of the same gender (e.g., David and Joab), consider referring to both characters by their proper names only.

Tip #5: Speak of Past Events as if They Are Happening Now

Using the present tense in your movements is an effective means of enhancing listenability. It engages listeners more when we say, "David enters the room," instead of "David entered the room."

I first learned of this technique twenty years ago. I had a Bible that put an asterisk after words like "said" in the Gospels. When I checked the footnotes, I learned that the asterisk meant that while those words are translated in my Bible in the past tense, the Gospel writers wrote them in the present tense. I couldn't understand at the time why they would use the present tense to speak of past events. I wondered if this made the Bible factually inaccurate! I've lightened up since then, and come to realize it's a great way to increase listeners' interest.

CHAPTER 7

Preach through the CUT (Part 2): Other Options

There are three alternatives to movements: summarize-without-reading, explain-as-you-read, and lead-ins. For some verses in a CUT, it is better to use one of these instead of a movement to illuminate the text and maintain an effective and varied pace for the sermon.

I've tried to give these alternatives understandable names. For example, when we summarize-without-reading, we preach through a set of verses by summarizing them only; we don't read them. To explain-as-you-read is to explain a verse or two as we're reading them. Lead-ins are a bit like movements, except we only illuminate a portion of the text before reading it because our goal is to explain it more fully after reading it.

Summarize-without-Reading

The most common alternative is to summarize-without-reading. As the name implies, it refers to places in the sermon where we summarize a set of verses without reading them. Although we'll usually summarize-without-reading some verses from most CUTs, the need for this alternative is most apparent when preaching longer ones like Genesis 2:4–3:24; 6:9–9:17; or 2 Samuel 11–12.

There are three times when the choice to summarize-without-reading can ensure an effective and varied pace. The first is when a CUT's length makes it necessary. A congregation may listen patiently to a one-hour sermon, but most preachers know it's not effective to do that.

The second time is when we want to move quickly to another set of verses or the next part of the sermon. After narrating David's first two attempts to use "legal means" to murder Uriah, it may be best to summarize the third attempt, even though the text elaborates heavily on that scheme and its use of messengers.

The third time is when a narrative provides complex information that would be more easily digested with a quick summary. For example, it would be difficult for many listeners to follow Nathan's parable to David in 2 Samuel 12:1–6, so it might be best to summarize-without-reading it, especially given the CUT's length.

When we summarize-without-reading, it's often best to keep it under fifty words. Some preachers find it difficult to leave out any textual nuance when they summarize-without-reading, but know that succinct ones tend to be more effective. All we need to do is capture the gist of the verses.

> **[Transition]** After Uriah proves to have more integrity when drunk than David has sober, David finds himself "0-for-2." He decides to use a different "legal means" to murder Uriah.
>
> **[SUMMARIZE-WITHOUT-READING]** David sends Uriah back to the battlefield with a note. Uriah doesn't know it, but it's his own death warrant. In the note, David instructs Joab, his top military commander, to put Uriah on the front lines and then pull his men back, ensuring Uriah's death. David's *plan* succeeds. Uriah's murdered "legally" [2 Samuel 11:14–25].

Nonetheless, let the text, the needs of the sermon, and the needs of the audience guide you. To summarize-without-reading Nathan's parable in 12:1–6 in fifty words would likely make it difficult for listeners to see the relationship between the parable and v. 7's "You are that man!"

> [SUMMARIZE-WITHOUT-READING] God dispatches Nathan the prophet to confront David. Nathan begins with a parable-in-disguise: "Hey David, I have a story for you. I want to get your thoughts on it. There are these two men. One is rich. The other poor. The rich man has everything. The poor man nothing. Nothing, but a little lamb. He loves that lamb. He treats it like family. One day, the rich man welcomes a visitor. However, the rich man doesn't want to feed the visitor from his own flock, so he steals the poor man's lamb. He cooks it and feeds it to the visitor. David, what do you make of that?"
>
> David's furious at the rich man. He curses and condemns him. The rich man's behavior is outrageous [2 Samuel 12:1–6].

Explain-as-You-Read

The second alternative is to explain-as-you-read. We do this by selecting *no more than two verses in a row* and explain them as we read them. This can be an effective way to enter the body of a sermon or to accentuate the drama of the text. However, avoid using it more than three times in a sermon; it would slow the pace of the sermon down too much. Often once or twice is enough, and sometimes it's not needed at all.

To explain-as-you-read, we must first state the verse number—or if entering a new chapter, both the chapter and verse. Preachers often neglect to say something like, "Look with me at verse 27," on the assumption that listeners know which verse(s) will be covered next, but that assumes too much. It also makes it difficult for listeners who hadn't been tracking with us perfectly to get back on track.

After providing the verse reference, begin to read its words. When we come to a word or phrase we want to explain or amplify, we do just that. Sometimes we'll comment right before we read a word or phrase and sometimes right after. The process continues until we've worked our way through those one or two verses.

First Verse of the CUT
When moving from Announce the Passage to the body of the sermon, it can be effective to explain-as-you-read the CUT's first verse. This is particularly the case if the first verse provides setting or background information, and the story's action begins in the second verse. When we enter the body of the sermon, it's a good idea to add a brief transition that includes a phrase like "As our story opens."

> [Transition] As our story opens, we find Abraham minding his own business.
>
> [EXPLAIN-AS-YOU-READ] Verse 1 begins, "After these things God tested Abraham." The word "tested," here, has the sense of stretching someone to their outer limits. Picture Abraham as a rubber band [grunt as hands stretch an imaginary rubber band].
>
> Verse 1 continues, "and [God] said to him, 'Abraham!' And he"—that is, Abraham—"said, 'Here I am.'" I'm here, Lord.

To Accentuate the Text's Drama
Explain-as-you-read can be an excellent way to change the sermon's pace, slow its tempo, or accentuate the drama inherent in a CUT. Choosing to explain-as-you-read can produce a powerful pause that

slows down the sermon for dramatic effect. It can be an excellent way to help listeners both understand and feel verses that are emotionally weighty.

> [EXPLAIN-AS-YOU-READ] Verse 26 tells us, "When the wife of Uriah heard that Uriah her husband was dead, she lamented over her husband." In that culture, you were expected to grieve publicly for a period of time. We can assume like anyone who loses a loved one, she grieved much longer, privately. Verse 27: "And when the mourning was over, David sent and brought her to his house, and she became his wife and bore him a son." David's cover-up is complete. His public image is intact. The public might have even seen David as a hero who saved a deceased military hero's wife from possible destitution.
>
> Yet we're left to wonder, *"Is this the kind of ambassador God will use to fulfill his plans?* Someone who abuses his power, covers up his tracks, and gets away with it? Where is God in all this?
>
> Despite the way things look, God has seen what's happened—and he's not happy. Look at the end of verse 27: "But the thing that David had done displeased the Lord."

Lead-In

The final and least frequently used alternative is the lead-in. While movements are designed to illuminate their verses, so that listeners will understand and feel their dynamics, lead-ins highlight only *an aspect* of their verses, because elaboration of those verses will be necessary after they are read. We use lead-ins when movements, no matter how well-crafted, would not enable listeners to comprehend a text or feel its rhetorical power for themselves. For this reason, they are also helpful for addressing highly unusual verses (e.g., Gen. 30:38–39; Josh. 10:13–14).

The idea is to prepare listeners for the explanation to come, by introducing them to it before the text is read—so that after the text's been read, they are prepared to hear more. For example, when reading Genesis 11:5, listeners would not be able to sense the reality check and sarcasm in it—not even with an effective movement. Therefore, a lead-in is used instead.

> [LEAD-IN] It's at this point we're given a heavy dose of reality and a good measure of sarcasm.
>
> [READ] Look at verse 5, "And the Lord came down to see the city and the tower, which the children of man had built."
>
> [EXPLAIN] Here the people are, here are so many today, defying God's redemptive plans, and thinking, "Where is your God?" Verse 5 hits us with a steady dose of reality: God is watching. He sees what we're doing. Make no mistake about it.
>
> Verse 5 also hits us with a good measure of sarcasm. The people were so proud of themselves: "Who else can build a tower that reaches into the heavens?" Yet verse 5 says that the Lord had to come way down just to see what they're doing.
>
> The picture, here, is of God sitting atop his lofty perch [stand on a chair]. It's as if God is saying, "Hey angels, I hear the folks at Shinar think they've got things figured out. I hear they're building a tower that'll reach way up into the sky. Do you see anything?"

> The angels reply, "You mean [squinting eyes and pointing down, as if trying to identify a speck of dust from a distance] right there? I think I see something." God replies, "That's it, right down there. I'm going to check it out."

It's worth noting that it's the diversity of choices in chapters 6–7 and in the rest of the book that make it so ten pastors, following closely the approach of this book, could preach very different sermons, even though their sermons are from the same CUT, and they agree on its basic message. Inevitably, some sermons would be better than others, but all would be accurate, relevant, clear—and to varying degrees, inspiring to listen to.

CHAPTER 8

STATE THE TAKE-HOME TRUTH

The THT is a timeless or contemporary expression of the OTM. It's also the organizing idea of the sermon, the single sentence on which the entire sermon hinges. Paul Scott Wilson is surely correct:

> Those who dismiss theme sentences make a . . . mistake. . . . A well-deployed thesis sentence can be a listener's best friend. . . . [Without it] no one really knows what the preacher is getting at. . . . Avoiding a thesis statement can be a form of tyranny, for the preacher demands that the listeners discover the preacher's meaning without offering what is needed.[1]

We've discussed how the THT, or the question it answers, affects both the introduction and movements or their alternatives. This chapter explains where to state the THT in the body of the sermon, and how to do it effectively. There are two options: (1) as we preach through the text, and (2) immediately after we preach through it.

---

1. Wilson, *Preaching and Homiletical Theory*, 23.

As We Preach through the Text

There comes a point toward the end of many OT narratives in which a verse or set of verses convey most or all of the THT, or at least serves as a climactic point at which listeners can see the THT in the text for themselves. For CUTs that have such a point, that's where we'll want to state the THT.

We don't simply state the THT, however. Specifically, we state it between a transition and a movement; and after the movement we read its verses. Here's a more visual way of saying the same thing:

- Transition to the THT.
- State the THT and immediately restate it.
- Provide a short movement of the verse(s) that are about to be read.
  → Read only the verses that clinch the THT.
  → Explain the verses just read (usually omitted).

In the transition, we need to sign-post what we're doing; we need to let listeners know what's about to happen. Although listeners should be very familiar with the question raised in the Focus because we've alluded to it regularly, we must raise it again, and tell listeners we've reached the point at which the question will be answered.

Next, we state the THT—and when we do, restate it. This means that we say essentially the same thing in different words, immediately after saying it the first time (i.e., the very next sentence). Hopefully, the question was restated in the Focus, and we can answer that restated question here, as well.

We then provide a brief movement and read its verses. Begin the movement by referring back to the THT with a statement like "We see this as . . ." and follow that up with a brief summary that indicates to listeners how they can see the THT in the verses.

> [Transition] It's at this point we discover what kind of ambassador, even an ambassador of Christ today, God will use to fulfill his plan of salvation. We discover who among us God will use to further the gospel.
>
> [THT] We discover God will use any ambassador to fulfill his plan of salvation, he will use us to further the gospel, even if we've gotten sidetracked by sin, if we will repent. If we will but turn back to him. But keep in mind: Sin brings discipline.
>
> [MOVEMENT] We see this as David responds with repentance, and Nathan assures him of God's forgiveness. But discipline remains.
>
> [READ] Read with me verses 13 and 14, "David said to Nathan, 'I have sinned against the LORD.' And Nathan said to David, 'The LORD also has put away your sin; you shall not die. Nevertheless, because by this deed you have utterly scorned the LORD, the child who is born to you shall die.'"

Here is another example in a sermon from Genesis 11:1–9:

> [Transition] As God, metaphorically, makes the long trek down, the Bible tells us we reach a pivotal point in human history. God must choose: Let the people thwart his redemptive plans or continue his redemptive plans by thwarting their plans. God chooses redemption. We have a God whose nature doesn't allow him to abandon his redemptive plans. His plans can't be thwarted.
>
> In the verses that follow, it becomes clear why we must align ourselves with God's redemptive plans.

> We discover the problem with making a name for ourselves, in defiance of God's plans.
>
> [THT] We should align ourselves with God's redemptive plans, because God's redemptive plans will prevail. It's futile to make a name for ourselves, because God will ultimately thwart our efforts.
>
> [MOVEMENT] This becomes clear as God responds to the people's defiance by giving them new languages:
>
> [READ] Let's read, beginning at verse 6, "⁶And the Lord said, 'Behold, they are one people, and they have all one language, and this is only the beginning of what they will do. And nothing that they propose to do will now be impossible for them. ⁷Come, let us go down and there confuse their language, so that they may not understand one another's speech.'"

When we state the THT before the CUT ends, it's important to finish preaching through the text. For example, we can't stop at 2 Samuel 12:14; there are seventeen verses left. Likewise, we shouldn't ignore Genesis 11:8–9 simply because we've stated the THT. However, neither can we spend much longer than five minutes preaching through the verses that remain. We reach a crescendo when we state the THT, and audience interest would wane if we were to continue to explain the text for longer than that.

Although the best way to preach through some or all of the remaining verses is often to summarize-without-reading, there are times when the verses that follow reinforce, or validate further, the THT. When that's the case, we should create movements for those verses, and make sure we use language from the THT in those movements:

> [MOVEMENT] The Lord's word comes true. The building stops. God's redemptive plans prevail, as the people disperse. They continue to fill the whole known world. In an ironic twist, the inhabitants of Shinar are *given* a name: Babel, meaning "confusion."
>
> [READ] Read with me verse 8 and 9, "So the Lord dispersed them from there over the face of all the earth, and they left off building the city. Therefore its name was called Babel, because there the Lord confused the language of all the earth. And from there the Lord dispersed them over the face of all the earth."

Preachers who are new to the skills of oral clarity sometimes worry that they sound redundant because they've referred to the THT a number of times within a few minutes, but listeners don't sense that at all. They're just glad they can follow the sermon; it's often a new experience for them. Listeners only feel preachers are being redundant when no good reason exists for why they are stating or restating an idea again, and preachers rarely do that.

After the THT has been stated and the text has been preached through, we move to the second phase of the body of the sermon. In the first phase, we preach through the text. In the second, we develop the THT—by helping listeners (buy and) apply, the THT.

Since the THT's been stated already, there is nothing new to say as we head into the second phase. Nonetheless, we must still make a smooth transition to the next phase, or else the sermon will have a momentary dead spot or awkward moment where listeners sense, "Okay, we've gone through the text, now what?"

The most effective way to make this transition is to remind listeners of the THT. Be sure to include language from the "official" version and its restatement. No, we're not going to sound redundant.

> [Transition] That God's redemptive plans will prevail has significant consequences for all of us.
>
> For one, if we ignore them, there will come a day when we realize that our greatest accomplishments, the name we've made for ourselves, the things we pride ourselves on the most, will be our undoing.

Here's another example:

> [Transition] We have a great God, do we not? Joy filled my heart this week at the confidence I can have, that you can have, that God will use us. We can get so down on ourselves. We can feel like we are the only ones we know with our particular struggle. And yet, God's willingness to use us is less about which sins sidetrack us and more about our willingness to own up to them. To repent and return to him.
>
> It was also a good reminder that God is not a doormat. He disciplines us. We are his children.

After We Preach through the Text

Sometimes there is no good opportunity to state the THT as we preach through the text. There may be no single go-to point in the CUT to clinch the THT, or that point may appear too early in the passage. When that occurs, we need to state the THT immediately after preaching through it.

Movements become doubly important in these sermons. They not only need to allude to the question in the Focus throughout, the words specific to the THT must appear prominently in them (or their alternatives). Listeners need to have already heard all the words of the THT, even if those words were never put together in the exact way they are in the THT. When listeners hear the THT, they need to have the distinct impression, "Yeah, that's right! I *did* see that in the text."

To state the THT after we've preached through the text, provide a transition that includes the question that was raised in the Focus. Notice that we *don't* say, "What's the Take-Home Truth?" It's that kind of odd sign-posting that draws too much attention to the sermon's inner workings. Rather, we raise the question the entire sermon has sought to answer. Listeners will perk up, knowing we have reached the point they have been anticipating. After the transition, state the THT and restate it immediately.

> **[Transition]** So then, Why must we remain grateful to God, even when trusting him results in hardship? Why is grumbling against God—his character and his will—out of line when things don't go our way?
>
> **[THT]** We must remain grateful because God has a proven track record of providing for the needs of his people. Our grumbling is out of line, because God has consistently provided us with everything we need.

CHAPTER 9

Help Listeners "Buy" the Take-Home Truth

Once we've preached through the CUT and stated the THT, it's often a good idea to help listeners overcome objections to the THT. We call this the "buy" section. It's an optional section; we don't always include it. But when included, it usually comes after the text has been preached and before the "application" section; in sermons from other genres, it could come after the explanation of each main point.

This section should not be confused with other places in the sermon where we may overcome objections. For example, when we come across hard-to-believe verses (e.g., Josh. 10:13–14; Gen. 30:38–39), we would do well to address any issues right then, as we preach through the text. Further, this section is not the place to handle doubts listeners may have about the THT's textual authority or validity. We must secure confidence in that as we preach through the text.

The buy section addresses one thing: objections to the THT itself, specifically those objections that would keep open-minded listeners from putting the THT into practice. We're looking to address objections arising from cognitive dissonance, where people reject, alter, or ignore an idea they consider plausible to alleviate the psychological discomfort that comes with accepting it.[1]

---

1. Harmon-Jones, *Encyclopedia of the Mind*, s.v. "Cognitive Dissonance."

That we distinguish between the buy and application sections for organizational purposes doesn't mean that objections can't be raised in the application section or that applications can't appear in the buy section. For example, our response to an objection in the buy section may include a Picture-Painting Application (PPA). Likewise, a PPA in the application section may implicitly help listeners "buy" the THT by showing them how to move past a worldly rationalization, so they can put the THT into practice.

The buy section can be the tipping point of the sermon. Some listeners may want to follow the THT, but are held back by unresolved questions. When we handle their objections effectively, they become free to put the THT into practice. However, listeners are not always aware during the sermon that they have these questions. Instead, their objections may exist as feelings that wouldn't become concrete thoughts until a week or two later. In some cases, listeners don't have doubts at all about a THT, but they *will* at some point—and we would do well to inoculate them in the sermon against those objections.

Two Components of Overcoming Objections

There are two parts to overcoming an objection: raising the objection and overcoming it. It seems easy enough, but it takes skill to do well. It's worth noting that we are not limited to overcoming one objection. Feel free to raise and respond to two or more. For example, a sermon on the responsibilities of working-age adults to their aging parents may need to overcome a number of objections.

Raise the Objection

Usually objections are raised in the form of a question. To ensure clarity and maintain the sermon's coherence, we must mention the THT when we raise an objection. This is another place where preachers new to the skills of oral clarity may worry that the THT will have been said too many times in the sermon, so they either omit the THT here or raise an objection to a principle other than the THT (which seems like a peculiar thing to do, but it happens).

This only confuses the audience, however. Listeners like it when the THT is stated plenty of times; they enjoy a seamless message. Further, raising an objection with a question that includes the THT regains the attention of those who've zoned out and gives them what they need to get back on track immediately.

We must also raise objections respectfully. We need to show we understand listeners' struggles the way they do, without a smidgen of judgment. We need to state them in ways that make listeners feel accepted, as people. We need to express objections fairly, in a way that makes them sound like the reasonable questions they are. Further, we need to avoid presumptuous statements like, "You're *probably* thinking. . . ." We may not think we intend to be rude with statements like that, but our word choice reveals how we think about the world, and listeners pick up on it.

Overcome the Objection

After raising an objection, we must overcome it. We don't want to be like politicians who respond to questions without answering them! Nor do we want to raise an objection, only to give a "deal with it" response. For example, I once heard a preacher raise an excellent objection in a sermon from an epistle: "I can't live by those standards! I can't run my life with the self-control of an Olympic athlete." Unfortunately, he then replied with, "Too bad—that's what the Bible teaches," and followed that up with a theological explanation of why people don't want to live a disciplined Christian life. His response not only lacked empathy; it didn't overcome the objection. The result: No one was helped.

There's another problem with a response like that: It's unfair emotionally. When we raise objections, listeners open their hearts, acknowledge their feelings, and feel more vulnerable. It's emotionally unfair to then shut them down with a condescending lecture.

Reasons People Don't Buy THTs from OT Narratives

Humans are a diverse and creative bunch. We have different personalities, life experiences, and agendas. From birth we all develop a unique personal emotional program, our best guess on how to navigate through life. For all of our uniqueness, however, there are only a few reasons open-minded people might hesitate to put a textually justified THT into practice, and typically only two of them come into play with THTs from OT narratives: either (1) they can't systematize it, or (2) they value something else even more.

They Can't Systematize It

Sometimes people hold off on integrating the THT into their life because it doesn't quite make sense to them. They may be confused about a cause-effect relationship. How could honoring our parents during our working years lead to a long life? Or, they may not understand how two statements could be true simultaneously. For example, how can God be good when he called Israel to purge the Canaanites from the Promised Land?

We answer objections like these by showing how the issue can be resolved. It's important, however, to think through our solutions. We don't want to answer one difficult question with a simplistic solution that raises three more. Fortunately, one of the major commentaries we selected may discuss potential solutions. Further, we need to preface tentative solutions with qualifiers like, "It's likely" or "It could be." In some cases, it can be powerful to say, "I don't know." Listeners are increasingly okay with unresolved tensions, and saying "I don't know" can give them the support they need to relax and trust God.

> **[BUY]** Some of us may be feeling, "Ben, I'm glad to know that when I fail to trust God, he will use me to further his plans, if I return to him. The problem is, I

don't know if I can trust God, if he disciplines people like that. The way he disciplined David. That's scary."

Friend, I'm with you. It would be a frightening thing, if God disciplined everyone like that.

The good news is that our passage doesn't suggest, doesn't even hint, that God would discipline us the same way. In fact, no passage in the Bible does.

God disciplined David in a way that was unique to David's situation. We don't have enough of the full picture to know exactly why God disciplined David that way, but God does. He sees the full picture. Sometimes, God acts in ways that are impossible for us to understand.

What we do know is God is a God of love. He is altogether good and righteous. He knows you, and he cares for you—deeply. He'd never tempt you, and I would say, he'd never discipline you beyond what you could bear. That's not the purpose of his discipline.

So I invite you to trust him. Press fully on into the faith. This auditorium is full of people who have done just that. God has disciplined all of them [big, warm smile], and they all still delight in his love for them.

They Value Something Else Even More

Listeners may not always feel an urgent need to follow the THT. They may feel that the THT's not a big deal, or that they'll get around to following it later. The need for a good grade may outweigh the need to be honest on a reading report. The desire to find a spouse may be more important than marrying within the faith or living a holy life.

To overcome these objections, we need to empathize with listeners and show them why following the THT is more desirable. We can do this by picturing real, potential outcomes. For example, we can show the positive benefits of following the THT and, possibly, the negative consequences of following the competing belief. Picturing positive benefits is often sufficient; however, if we choose to picture negative consequences, we need to then inspire our listeners with something positive.

When we picture potential outcomes, it's crucial to not say with certainty what will happen. We can see how true this is by looking at our own ministries. We've all adopted various programs and models that assured us of results—vast numbers will be saved, the church will be transformed, etc.—that never panned out. Listeners, even more than pastors, are not only tired of success formulas; they are harmed by them.

> [BUY] Some of us might feel, "Ben, I get what you're saying about aligning myself with God's redemptive plans. I'm no model of virtue at work. I can be rude. I curse. I also know I work too many hours.
>
> "Here's the thing: I made a promise to myself when my husband left me to raise my kids alone ten years ago: Never be dependent on a man. I've achieved that. I've worked hard to get where I am. I don't want to let go."
>
> I can appreciate your situation, and God bless you for all you do for your kids. Friend, God loves you and wants what's best for you. He's called us to trust him, and unlike those who have hurt you, he will never leave you or forsake you.
>
> Nonetheless, we both know the business world can only offer the illusion of security. Surely you've known

> of executives who've given all and lost everything on account of layoffs, an ethical lapse, or illness.
>
> God wants you on the winning team. He wants you to trust Christ completely. I feel sad to think that like those at Babel, the one thing you were most proud of could become your undoing. How wonderful would it be if your children, as they head toward adulthood, see your faithfulness and become full-fledged members of God's team as well?
>
> Be courageous. If that means less hours with less pay, take that step of faith. If that means transitioning to a new position, take that step. Whatever it is, align yourself with God's redemptive plans.

Here's another example:

> [BUY] But some of us are in a tough spot. You see from our passage that our faithfulness matters, because it's a public display of God's holiness. Our trust in him is a testimony to his holiness.
>
> Maybe you're in your thirties. You want to get married. You want to have kids. Time's running out. You went to the church's singles group, and well . . . you weren't that impressed.
>
> You feel pressure to go with your friends to bars or parties to meet people. Maybe you've started dating someone, a friend of a friend or a co-worker. He's not a Christian, but at least he's got a job! He's funny. He's good to you. Testifying to God's holiness feels too restricting, too theoretical.

Friend, while it's true that displaying God's holiness is an end in itself, it's also true that it benefits us. Our choices have consequences. For Moses, God kept him from entering the Promised Land. All that work, and he didn't enter it.

I can't tell you how God will discipline you, or what the consequences will be if you marry an unbeliever, but I can share what often happens: In most cases, people's relationship with Christ never completely recovers.

Suppose you embrace a deeper faith commitment after you marry an unbeliever. It may cause marital strife. Your spouse didn't sign up to marry someone of deep faith. And what about your kids? It's common for kids who grow up with one parent outside of the faith to never develop a deep walk with God. Many never come to faith in Christ at all.

And for all you know, Mr. Right—someone who desires to display God's holiness—could be on his way. Yet, if our heart's not ready, we could stare at them and never see them.

CHAPTER 10

Develop Picture-Painting Applications

The application section comes after, or in place of, the buy section. Since sermons from OT narratives will almost always proclaim a single idea that arises after consideration of the entire CUT, application needs to wait until after the text has been preached through. Nonetheless, the entire sermon should be relevant in the sense of us making connections to real life throughout.

Preaching is about life change. Using the Bible and a few illustrations—stories, props, humor, metaphors, etc.—God can work through us to convince and inspire listeners to want to follow the THT. Excellent sermons, however, go further. They provide concrete application. They show listeners what it looks like to put the theology of the text into practice.

Consider Jason and Suzy. They are one of your favorite couples at the church. Married for fourteen years, they've been attending for the last eight. They have two children, ages four and eight. They make a good family. They attend weekly, take notes enthusiastically, and lead a midweek small group. If anyone benefits from your sermons, it's them.

One Tuesday you receive a call. "Pastor, we need to meet with you. Our marriage is on the verge of collapse. Help!" You meet with them the next day. You learn that Jason's shutting down, and it's driving Suzy crazy. When they try to communicate, it quickly turns ugly.

How effective would it be at this point to share a few Bible verses, remind them that "God calls us to love our spouses, even when it's difficult," and send them home? It wouldn't! Why? It's not because it's not true. And it's not because they don't believe it—they do. It's because they don't know what it looks like to do it.

Listeners need us to show them what it looks like to put the THT into practice. They need help moving from abstract principle to concrete theological practice. If we are honest with ourselves, we'll realize that our own lives testify to this truth. Sunukjian writes:

> The listeners usually will not make [the applications] for themselves. I know from my own experience when I'm on vacation and listening to another preacher. At the end of his message—when the music is playing, the congregation is dismissed, and people are trying to step past me to get to the aisle—if he hasn't given me some concrete pictures of how the truth bears on my life, I don't stay seated in my chair, blocking others. . . . No. I rise like the others, turn to my wife, and say, "You want to get hamburgers or pizza? You get the girls; I'll get the boys. I'll meet you at the car."[1]

Think about it this way: If we spend ten to twenty hours in focused sermon preparation and cannot figure out concrete ways to apply the message, what is the likelihood that listeners will? Not likely, not even with sermon notes or message-based small groups. Many listeners do not take notes, and most that do put them in the trash or ignore them. Further, less than fifty percent of the congregation attends midweek small groups and the "applications" discussed in them may miss the mark. Yes, God works, sometimes mightily, through the coruscating effects of the sermon. Still, the only reliable way to ensure listeners see how the THT can be lived out is if we show them.

Picture-painting applications (PPAs) are an effective way to develop concrete application. They place listeners in real-life

---

1. Sunukjian, *Invitation to Biblical Preaching*, 111.

situations and show how the THT can be lived out in them. The rest of this chapter discusses initial objections to PPAs, keys to their effectiveness, and a template for creating them. It also includes three ways to modify the template, according to the needs of the listeners and sermon.

Initial Objections to PPAs

Three objections are often raised against PPAs. First, some feel it's the Holy Spirit's job to make application. This assumes the untenable position that we are somehow not instruments of the Spirit when we make application—even when, as preachers, we are exercising our Spirit-ual gifting. The Bible, however, teaches that we are God's ambassadors and that God makes his appeal through us (2 Cor. 5:20). It also calls us to patiently "reprove, rebuke, and exhort" (2 Tim. 4:2). Are we to suppose, without scriptural support, that God ceases to work through us when we make concrete sermon application? And, if only the Holy Spirit can make application, why is it acceptable to provide concrete application in pastoral counseling, marriage and parenting classes, and recovery ministries?

Second, others express concern that we may miss someone. In spite of the irony—we miss *everyone* when our application remains at the abstract level—it's a reasonable concern. In applying a text to a retired businessman, have we now failed to minister to the struggling college student or single mother? No, because listeners adjust PPAs to fit their situation. For example, retired teachers and others on a fixed income or tight budget make the necessary mental adjustments when they hear PPAs designed for retired businessmen. Additionally, most people expect to retire one day or have a relative who is already retired, so they take note. Even if we miss someone completely, we have at least allowed that person to appreciate the struggles of others in a way that holds their interest. And remember, we can always create multiple PPAs for each sermon!

Third, some aren't sure if they can fit PPAs into their sermons; we only have so much time. PPAs vary in length—usually one to four minutes—depending on whether we follow the full template or use a shorter variation. Most thirty-minute sermons, however, have plenty of time for multiple PPAs, so long as we preach unified, focused messages that avoid needless cross-referencing.

Keys to Effectiveness

Before we move on to the PPA template and its variations, let's discuss some key ingredients for crafting effective ones.

Relax
Relaxation is crucial to sermon preparation, especially when it comes to the hardest part: concrete application. We need to accept that coming up with PPAs will take longer than we want to give it, especially when we're new to creating them. Don't worry about creating perfect PPAs. By following the template or one of its variations closely, we'll find that "okay" PPAs are effective.

Tie It to the Take-Home Truth
We've spent hours determining the THT and revising its wording. Don't jettison it—apply it. Preachers who are new to PPAs often find one reason or another to apply a different principle. For example, if the THT is, "God will ensure there are always people who worship him," *don't* seek to apply a different concept by transitioning with, "What does it look like to trust in God's perfect timing when it comes to witnessing?" It makes no sense to apply a different principle; the text doesn't teach it, and the rest of the sermon never develops it.

Identify Applicable Situations
To come up with applicable situations, create and use a Life Situation Grid or form an Application Team. To use a Life Situation

Grid, such as the basic one that follows, circle characteristics from multiple columns, and then ask, "For someone in this situation, when would the THT be applicable?"[2]

Gender & Age	Cultural Identity	Employment Status	Job Level	Marital Status	Kids' Ages	Regular Activities
M	African	Home-maker	Entry	Single	< 2	Ministry
F	American	Part-Time	Gen.	Dating	2–4	Min. Ldr.
8–13	Arabian	Full-Time	Office	Engaged	4–6	Driving
13–15	Armenian	Laid Off	Trade	Newlywed	7–10	Chores
15–18	Chinese	Fired	Sales	Married	10–11	Bills
18–25	Korean	Retired	Exec.	Remarried	Jr High	Taxes
25–35	Persian		Owner	Divorced	HS	Hobbies
35–50				Widowed	College	Kids' Activities
50–65	1st Gen.				Grown	
65+	2nd Gen.					

Forming an Application Team can also be helpful. Preachers, stressed and under time constraints, may struggle to think of scenarios that the THT affects. Others, however, do not have the same pressures and may think of them easily. Application Teams can be especially helpful in multi-ethnic churches, where preachers serve listeners with significantly different cultural perspectives, life experiences, and felt needs. They can also prove helpful in churches that consist of first- and second-generation immigrants from the same ethnic background.

To form an Application Team, ask congregants of diverse ages and backgrounds if it would be okay to call or email them occasionally to ask when or how a biblical concept might apply.

---

2. Consider creating a more detailed Life Situation Grid with the help of Sunukjian, *Invitation to Biblical Preaching*, 113–17.

When team members share scenarios for application, ask them questions to uncover the underlying psychological or cultural dynamics. Like many of the exegetical discoveries made in sermon preparation, much of this cultural exegesis will not make it into the PPA, but all of it will benefit it. While team members may not always come up with scenarios that fit the THT precisely—application is exacting work—they will usually come up with something close enough, so that with a little modification their scenarios will fit.

Be Realistic
Listeners may feel we're Bible experts, but they consider themselves experts on real life. When we show how the Bible applies to specific situations, listeners run what we say—however unconsciously—through a reality filter. The more realistic the PPA, the greater is its effectiveness. Therefore, use real situations and common speech, not "religious speak." Work plausibly from problem to solution, and make the possible outcomes and long-term benefits believable. That said, err on the side of rationality. In narrating situations where faithfulness is difficult, it would be counterproductive to present people as irrational, even if it would be realistic to do so.

Show More Than Tell
We "tell" when we narrate with description ("You walk toward your room."). We "show" when we narrate with dialogue, physical movement, or action ("Your eyes widen. Your heart races. You take a step, then another."). Showing is more engaging. It activates listeners' imagination. It involves them in the application. It reaches the heart quicker. It's more effective to say, "I'm gonna set him straight" than "You decide to set him straight."

Telling is helpful, however, when we want to move quickly to a more important point in the PPA. Over time, develop the ability to "do one or the other, but not both." For example, we should either open our eyes wide, or say, "Your eyes open"—not both.

Template

What follows is a template for creating PPAs. At the end, I include three ways to modify it to fit the needs of the sermon. This template follows the standard dynamics of plot. The final element—the possible outcomes and long-term benefit—presents a realistic, but necessarily tentative, conclusion that is designed to embed an additional layer of hope into listeners' hearts. A running example, which incorporates the preceding five key ingredients, is used to illustrate each element.

Transition

Prepare listeners for a PPA with an effective transition. Effective transitions gain or regain listeners' attention, and enable those who have zoned out to immediately get back on track. Include the THT, and inform listeners of what is about to happen, either in the form of a statement (e.g., "Let's see what it looks like to …") or a question (e.g., "What does/might it look like to …"). It can also be helpful to orient listeners to the PPA by providing a brief description of the person it most directly addresses. End the transition with something like "Imagine," "Suppose," or "Picture this."

> [APPLY] How might the fact that "God will use us to fulfill his plan of salvation, but sin brings discipline" affect our lives? Maybe you're a dad who's concerned about how your kids will be able to afford college one day. Imagine:

Setting

Begin with a peaceful introduction. Activate listeners' imaginations, and orient them to the PPA's time and location. Involve the five senses. What do they see, hear, touch, taste, and smell? How do they feel? Minimize description. Use action, dialogue, and physical movement.

> Your eyes open. It's Saturday morning. [squinting] "7 am?!" [vocal grogginess turns into an optimistic smile] "Nothing coffee can't fix!" You head to the kitchen, kiss your wife, grab a cup of joe, and join the kids for breakfast. "You guys ready to play baseball today?" [Kids' reply:] "Of course, Dad."

Problem

At this point, introduce a trial, test, opportunity, or temptation to establish relevance and hold interest. It should be a situation people actually face, one that the THT applies to, and one in which the normal response is the wrong one. It should leave them feeling, "Ooh, that's a tough one," or "I know that one."

> Two hours later, you're driving to your oldest son's baseball game. He's thirteen. You think about college and finances: "The only way he can afford college is if he gets a sports scholarship. He's doing okay, but he's got to improve. He's got to practice more."
>
> The game begins. You notice he's batting seventh. In his first at-bat, he strikes out. On his second at-bat, he grounds out. Ditto on the third. You're frustrated.

Rationalization

Next, construct a worldly, but reasonable response. Build a quality case for the worldly response. Quality rationalizations increase a PPA's effectiveness in three ways. First, they add to the preacher's credibility, because they show that the preacher understands the challenges of real life. Second, they increase listeners' interest. Third, they make the biblical response more compelling because it proves to be more satisfying than its worldly alternative.

> After the game, as you head to the car together, you resolve to shoot straight with your son. He needs to know how this college thing works. You put on a calm smile. You'll walk right up next to him, so no one else will be able to hear what you're about to say. You adjust your vocal chords, ready to say with a harsh tone, "Why don't you get it? You need to stop goofing around after school and start practicing. College is expensive. If I can't afford it, you can't afford it. You've got to get a baseball scholarship. You wanna go to college, you wanna be somebody, don't you?"

Plot Twist
Right when it seems the rationalization will win the day, listeners are reminded of the THT.

> But then the thought arises, "God will use me to fulfill his plan of salvation, as long as I keep coming back to him, but sin brings discipline." You reflect: "If I take the next few years to ruin my relationship with my son over a baseball scholarship, God may still find a way to use me, but what will it cost me? I could lose my son. I could ruin my testimony. I don't want that."

Biblical Response
It's now time to resolve the rationalization—not the problem. The biblical response narrates steps that can be taken to put the THT into practice. Avoid solving the problem, arguing against the rationalization, or making the situation look like one big misunderstanding.

> "Lord, all I want is to give my kids a chance to succeed in life, but you're right. I can't do it by provoking my son's anger. You know what's best, and there's no need to invite your discipline. Give me wisdom."

> As you continue to walk to the car, you relax. Your frustration lessens. As you open the trunk, you look at your son and say, "It was a good game today." "Dad, it was a terrible game. I never even reached first base. I'm never gonna get a scholarship to college." "Maybe. Maybe not. Let's trust God, and see what happens. You don't need a scholarship to be great in God's eyes or mine." "Thanks, Dad."

Possible Outcome(s) and Long-Term Benefit

Bring PPAs to a soul-satisfying end by providing one or two immediate outcomes and a long-term benefit, but qualify them with "possible" language—we are not God, after all. In some PPAs, we may want to admit we don't know how things will turn out. Before moving on to the long-term benefit, share something *certain* about the nature of the biblical response, or God's reaction to it.

End the PPA with a possible long-term benefit. Try to make it an earthly benefit, some two to twenty years out. Make it relational. You could show how the biblical response positively affected another person (e.g., an unbeliever or co-worker) who saw what happened. In some cases, that person may not have been in the PPA up until that point.

> I can't tell you whether your son will get a scholarship or not. What I can tell you is that, at that moment, God used you to fulfill his plan of salvation. God used you to bring your son closer to Jesus.
>
> We never know what our faithfulness will lead to. You gave your son's teammate a ride home from the game that day. He's a good kid, but he's had a rough life. In ten years, he might see you around town and say, "Do you remember that time you said that no

> son of yours needs a scholarship to be great in your eyes or God's? When I heard that, I thought, 'If God can make someone into a dad like that, then I need God in my life. Thanks.'"

Variations
The purpose of the template above is to help us craft excellent applications, and not to suggest that following it exactly is the only way that an application can be effective. What follows are variations to the template. Feel free to create new variations. Variations enable us to address a wider range of problems and include more concrete application in each sermon.

Half & Half
This variation was mentioned in the discussion of the Engage stage of the introduction. It involves providing the first half of a PPA—the setting, problem, and rationalization—in the introduction and the rest of the PPA in the application section. It can be powerful to probe one or more difficult situations early in the sermon, and then call them back at this point to address them further. When we call them back, we could say something like, "Thinking back to the [blank] situation from earlier, how might we handle [one sentence summary of the situation]? What would it look like to [THT]?" And then pick up the PPA, starting with the plot twist.

Pre-Existing Situations
Not all problems arise in the moment. Some have been around for a while and may appear dormant, such as lingering anger felt by adult children toward their parents that dates back to childhood. To address situations like these, replace the setting, problem, rationalization, and plot twist with a description of the pre-existing situation, and say something like, "What would it look like to [THT]?" Then, follow the template starting with the biblical response.

[APPLY] Maybe you're a retired [Christian] businessman. What can you do to more fully align yourself with God's redemptive plans? Consider growing your relationship with your adult children.

[Description of Pre-existing Situation] The reality is that many of us have adult children whose faith is weak or nonexistent, and it stems from decades old parent-child tensions.

Dads, your adult children are still trying to impress you. They still want you to delight in them. Even billionaire Ted Turner admitted that recently—and his dad passed away decades ago.

[Biblical Response] Give your kids a call. Invite them to over to the house for lunch, one on one. If they live across the county, fly out to see them.

Be vulnerable. Share with them. If your son or daughter feels—or worse yet, doesn't feel but should—that you spent too much time at work and not enough with them growing up, share with them, "Hey, I wanted to get together with you today to say sorry for not valuing time with you like I should have when you were growing up. I want you to know: I delight in you more than I can express. When you were growing up I was too caught up trying to make it in this world."

Of course, don't stop at that conversation. Commit yourself to developing a deep, vulnerable, non-defensive relationship with them.

[Possible Outcome(s) and Long-term Benefit] I can't tell

> you how they'll respond. Humans are unpredictable. Your son might break down and cry. Your daughter might launch into a tirade of everything she's still hurt by.
>
> What I can tell you is the more you develop a deep, vulnerable relationship with them, the more you are aligning yourself with God's redemptive plans. The more you are participating in his plan to bring people to himself.
>
> And who knows, you may find that because you took those steps, the faith will be strong in your family for generations.

Compact

Full PPAs take time—anywhere from two to four minutes. They are worth every second. An excellent way to include more PPAs is to develop shorter, more descriptive ones. Compact PPAs tend to be about twelve sentences long. To create them, refer back to the THT and then, in one to four sentences each: (1) combine the setting and problem, (2) give the rationalization, and (3) combine the plot twist and biblical response. The possible outcome(s) and long-term benefit are optional.

> [APPLY] When might it be crucial to remember that "God will ensure there will always be people who worship him?" Some of us are in high school.
>
> [Setting & Problem] When you started high school you might have thought, "I'm going to be a light for Christ." But now you're discouraged. Almost no one's a Christian. Your friends may even think the Bible's irrelevant. Outdated.

[**Rationalization**] You may think to yourself, "If no one else believes, why should I? Maybe I'm the fool?"

[**Plot Twist & Biblical Response**] But then you remember, "God will ensure there will always be people who worship him." You're proof of that! You realize you're not alone. The Christian faith will never die out. You relax, and press on with a smile, confident that God knows what he's doing.

CHAPTER 11

Move to Christ

If we were to ask a group of pastors if it's important to preach Christ, the resounding answer would be "Yes!" If we were to ask them how to do that from OT narratives, they would give a variety of answers. Some might say we implicitly preach Christ, even in sermons that never mention him; the worship service makes that clear.

Other pastors would say we must explicitly preach Christ in every sermon, but that's where the agreement would end. Some would be satisfied so long as Christ is mentioned somewhere in the sermon. Another subset would say Christ is secretly or latently taught in every passage; we must find him and preach him. Some would say Christ is not taught in every passage, but that we should use creative means *à la* the NT to preach him anyway. A few explicitly affirm what is often implicit or accidental in many approaches: The sermon should center on Christ, to the neglect or misinterpretation of the text and its message.

Our look at the issue centers on two questions. First, what does the Bible mean by "preaching Christ"? Second, how can we make a seamless move to Christ?

The first question concerns the difference between God's commands and what we personally feel is a good idea. Anyone can advance a position, but unless the Bible teaches it, that position has no authority over us. For example, I think of one prominent

Christ-centered approach and wonder if it's a good idea for a passage that teaches, "Cleanse yourself from all unrighteousness," to word its main point this way: "God provides our righteousness" or "Confess that God provides the righteousness you lack"—or else add a main point like, "Depend on God to fulfill all righteousness."[1]

The second question seeks to discern ways to move to Christ faithfully without muddying the sermon. God inspired each CUT uniquely and with a specific theological message. If we move to Christ, but fail to communicate the message of the text, listeners may never get another opportunity to hear that CUT's Spirit-inspired message. The problem is compounded, if our methods for moving to Christ cause listeners to regularly miss the text's message.

What Does the Bible Mean by "Preaching Christ"?

Many approaches—with their rules and regulations—abound concerning the "right" way to preach Christ. They are typically difficult to implement, and most who adhere to a specific approach don't realize they aren't practicing it properly. I would suggest this says more about the approach than it does about those who try to follow it. What matters is what the Bible means by preaching Christ, for we have no right to insist someone preach Christ in a way that differs from what the Bible requires; that's legalism.

As we'll see below, preaching Christ simply means that our preaching, especially from the OT, must reflect New Covenant realities brought about by Jesus Christ; what we preach must be compatible with the New Covenant. This would mean, for example, that we can't preach an OT narrative's OTM unless every aspect of it carries over into the New Covenant. That's why we preach the THT, which replaces the OTM's Old Covenant-specific terms with their timeless or New Covenant-specific equivalents. Sidney Greidanus, the leading authority on preaching Christ, writes:

---

1. Chapell, *Christ-Centered Preaching*, 309–10.

> Preaching Christ means different things to different people. . . . According to the New Testament, preaching Christ is preaching Jesus of Nazareth as the climax of God's revelation of himself. Preaching Christ from the Old Testament is to preach sermons that authentically integrate the message of the Old Testament text with the climax of God's revelation in the person, work, and/or teaching of Jesus Christ as revealed in the New Testament.[2]

We are free to do more than that, but we're not in a position to require or guilt others into going beyond that. We'll arrive at this biblical understanding by examining the concept of preaching Christ in the Gospels, Acts, and relevant sections of the epistles.

Preaching Christ in the Gospels

While the Gospels do not use the phrase "preach/proclaim Christ," they contribute to the discussion through their use of the OT, and in key verses that address either the extent to which Christ is found in the OT or the influence of the New Covenant for preaching the OT.

The Use of the OT in the Gospels

Preachers often argue for their particular method of preaching Christ by arguing that it reflects the way the Gospels use the OT. A must-have volume, *Commentary on the New Testament Use of the Old Testament* edited by Gregory Beale and D. A. Carson, shows that the Gospel writers use the OT in a variety of ways, and that some of them are creative by our standards.

As the argument goes, we must follow the model or methods of the Gospel writers in our preaching from the OT. However, the argument fails for two reasons. First, that the Gospels use OT proof texts for evangelistic purposes doesn't mean that we must do the

---

2. Greidanus, "The Necessity of Preaching Christ Also from Old Testament Texts," 190–91.

same when preaching from CUTs of the OT. This is the issue of comparable particulars.[3]

The primary purpose of the Gospels is to prove that Jesus is the Messiah. Mark establishes this purpose up front in 1:1: "The beginning of the gospel of Jesus Christ, the Son of God." So do Matthew (1:1, 17) and Luke (1:1–4). John makes it explicit later in his Gospel: "Now Jesus did many other signs . . . but these are written so that you may believe that Jesus is the Christ, the Son of God, and that by believing you may have life in his name" (20:30–31).

We should expect the Gospels to use the OT this way; we would too in sermons that proclaim how some OT passages foretell of Jesus. Given their purpose, it would be strange if the Gospels were expositions of OT CUTs. Therefore, it's a stretch to claim that preachers today must follow the Gospels' evangelistic proof-texting practices or methods in most sermons from the OT.

Second, it's worth noting that the interpretive methods the Gospel writers used are neither authoritative nor binding on us, just as no other belief or practice that influenced the formation of the Gospels is either, unless the Bible taught that it was.

Extent to Which Christ Is Found in the OT

Another reason people give for their approach to preaching Christ is their belief that the Gospels teach that Christ is taught in every verse or passage of the OT. The two passages used to support this position are John 5:39 and Luke 24:27. However, a close look at them reveals that they teach Christ is taught or testified to in many—but not all or necessarily even most—OT passages.

Let's look first at John 5:39. There are two clues that this verse— "You search the Scriptures because you think that in them you have eternal life; and it is they that bear witness about me"—does not teach that all OT passages "bear witness," or "testify," to Jesus. The

---

3. See Fee and Stuart, *How to Read the Bible for All Its Worth*, 78–83. Although they address the issue in the context of the Epistles, they expect us to see its significance for the general task of theological analysis and application of biblical texts.

first is that the phrase "the Scriptures" (the plural forms of *graphē*), which is used twenty times in the NT, never refers to every verse or passage of Scripture. It can refer to Scripture in general (Acts 18:24; Rom. 1:2; 15:4; 16:26), various parts of Scripture (Luke 24:27, 32, 45; Acts 17:2; 18:28), non-Pauline Scriptures (2 Peter 3:16), specific passages related to a theological debate or teaching (Matt. 22:29; Mark 12:24; Acts 17:11; 1 Cor. 15:3–4), or even one prophecy (Matt. 21:42; 26:54–56; Mark 14:49). The latter verses are interesting because they speak of one prophecy fulfilling "the Scriptures." These verses are a good reminder of the need to avoid overliteralization, and to interpret texts on their own terms.[4]

The second clue comes a few verses later in vv. 45–46, where Jesus clarifies the meaning of v. 39's "the Scriptures . . . bear witness." What he says does not indicate that he has every verse or passage in mind, but a limited number of passages from the books of Moses (i.e., the Pentateuch). As he says in v. 46, "If you believed Moses, you would believe me; for he wrote of me." Thus Fee and Stuart are correct; Jesus "obviously was *not* speaking about every short individual passage of the Old Testament."[5]

Let's look now at the second passage, Luke 24:27. There are three clues that this verse—"And beginning with Moses and all the Prophets, he [Jesus] interpreted to them in all the Scriptures the things concerning himself"—does not suggest that Christ is in every OT passage. First, the short trip from Emmaus to Jerusalem didn't allow enough time for Christ to teach about himself from every OT passage. The trip was about seven miles long, and Jesus joined them partway through (vv. 13–15). At the standard walking rate of fifteen minutes per mile, they walked for less than two hours. Let's extend that generously to four hours, to allow for the possibility of a circuitous route and poor road conditions. Given that it typically takes two hours to read Genesis and at least thirty hours to

---

4. A study of the singular forms of *graphē* ("the Scripture") yields the same conclusion.
5. Fee and Stuart, *How to Read the Bible for All Its Worth*, 96.

read the OT, it's far-fetched to think that Luke would indicate that Jesus taught about himself from every, or anything close to most, OT passages in that short trip.

Second, the idea that Luke had every OT passage in mind is doubtful also because it's unlikely that Jesus or his companions would have had a complete set of OT scrolls on them. Owning, much less walking with, a full-set of OT scrolls was rare. It's more likely, then, that their discussions depended largely on their shared knowledge or memory of the OT, and thus it's improbable that every, or even most, OT passages would have been discussed.

Third, a corresponding verse in the same CUT, v. 44, clarifies that "all the Scriptures" in v. 27 means something akin to "all of the OT's macro-divisions." Verse 44 reads, "Then he [Jesus] said to them, 'These are my words that I spoke to you while I was still with you, that everything written *about me* in the Law of Moses and the Prophets and the Psalms must be fulfilled.'" So then, while v. 27 teaches that many passages in the OT proclaim Christ, it doesn't teach that all, or even most, do.

Jesus on the Influence of the New Covenant for Preaching from the OT

A significant issue for preaching Christ is the impact of the New Covenant. While Jesus never implied that we should preach only his person or work, he did teach that Old Covenant-specific concepts must be preached in light of New Covenant realities.

In Luke 22:20, Jesus states that he was establishing the New Covenant (cf. Matthew 26:27–28; Mark 14:24), which Hebrews 8:6–13 indicates is a fulfillment of Jeremiah 31:31–34. The New Covenant was necessary because the Old Covenant was fulfilled by Christ (Matt. 5:17). The New Covenant brought with it progressive revelation concerning, most significantly, Jesus Christ as Messiah and also knowledge of how the New Covenant continues, discontinues, expands, or develops the Old Covenant.

In Matthew 13:52, Jesus speaks of the relationship of the New Covenant to the Old: "And he said to them, 'Therefore every scribe who has been trained for the kingdom of heaven [i.e., a disciple] is like a master of a house, who brings out of his treasure what is new and what is old.'" Commenting on this verse, Keener writes, "Jesus expects his disciples to build on both the biblical teachings that had come before him and on his gospel of the kingdom."[6] Blomberg adds, "Jesus probably means that as his disciples teach God's will, they will be drawing out the meaning of the Hebrew Scriptures ('things old'), while showing how they are fulfilled and apply in the kingdom age ('things new')."[7]

Therefore, Jesus' approach is much simpler than many realize. In practice, we faithfully preach the OT, indeed Christ, so long as we express Old Covenant-specific concepts in the OTM as timeless or New Covenant ones in the THT. This is essentially how Christ was preached in 1 Peter 2:9–10, where New Covenant believers are equated with the Old Covenant-specific concepts of Israel and priests.[8] We do the same when we transition from the "Davidic Covenant" in the OTM of 2 Samuel 11–12 to "plan of salvation" in the THT. We are free to use other legitimate ways to move to Christ, but that's all the Gospels—and as we'll see, the NT—require us to do to preach Christ from the OT.

Preaching Christ in Acts

Acts develops the concept, "preaching Christ," in the context of the early church's evangelistic outreach. The book expresses it in a number of ways, and they are all synonymous with the gospel message, as Jesus formulates it in Acts' companion volume, Luke, specifically Luke 24:45–47.

Preaching Christ in Acts 5:42 is referred to as "preaching that the Christ is Jesus." In 6:2, 8:4, and 15:35, it's "preaching the word." In 8:12, it's "preach[ing the] good news about the kingdom of God and the name of Jesus Christ." In 8:25, 8:40, 14:7, 14:21,

---

6. Keener, *A Commentary on the Gospel of Matthew*, 393.
7. Blomberg, *Matthew*, 225.
8. Similarly Klein, Blomberg, and Hubbard, 496.

and 16:10, it's "preach[ing] the gospel." In 9:27–28, twice it's "preach[ing] boldly in the name of Jesus." In 10:36, it's "preaching good news of peace through Jesus Christ." In 10:42, it's a command "to preach to the people and to testify that he [Jesus] is the one appointed by God to be judge of the living and the dead." In 17:18, it's "preaching Jesus and the resurrection." In 20:24, it's "testify[ing] to the gospel of the grace of God."

Therefore, the contribution of Acts to the concept of "preaching Christ" is that our *evangelistic messages* must center on Christ and the gospel, in keeping with the New Covenant that was inaugurated by Jesus. However, Acts does not address how to preach Christ from CUTs of the OT.

Preaching Christ in 1–2 Corinthians

The books of 1–2 Corinthians play a central role in discussions about preaching Christ. In 1 Corinthians 1:23, Paul writes, "but we preach Christ crucified." In 2:2, he adds, "For I decided to know nothing among you except Jesus Christ and him crucified." Later, Paul tells the Corinthians, "For what we proclaim is not ourselves, but Jesus Christ as Lord" (2 Cor. 4:5). In these verses, Paul is not requiring anything more than what the Gospels or Acts require concerning the preaching of Christ.

Paul is addressing his own evangelistic preaching and the problems the Corinthians had with it. Paul wasn't a grand showman like the Sophists they preferred (2 Cor. 4:2–3; 11:1–6). They didn't find his troubles and poverty impressive (1:8, 15–17; 11:9). They wanted to drop the resurrection as part of the gospel message because it wasn't popular culturally (1 Cor. 1:18–19; 15:1–2, 12–19, 35–36). Preaching Christ in 1–2 Corinthians means, therefore, that our evangelistic messages must center on Christ, his crucifixion and resurrection (1 Cor. 15:3–4; 2 Cor. 11:4–5).

Preaching Christ in Colossians

Colossians 1:28 makes plain what is implicit in every NT letter: Preaching Christ involves more than the proclamation of the gospel message. It also includes teaching theology and ethics that comport with the New Covenant. It reads, "Him we proclaim, warning everyone and teaching everyone with all wisdom, that we may present everyone mature in Christ."

It's significant that Paul explicitly states this expanded view of preaching Christ in Colossians. The Colossians were tempted to embrace Old Covenant-specific theology and ethics (2:16). Notice, however, that Paul doesn't respond by saying something to the effect of, "we preach only the person or work of Jesus Christ." Instead, he says in essence that he proclaims also New Covenant theology and ethics, so that believers can move beyond conversion to a mature Christian faith and life.

While it doesn't surprise us that Paul preaches more than the person or work of Christ, what may surprise us is that means our notion of "preaching Christ" must expand beyond that to include New Covenant theology and practice (cf. 2 Tim. 3:16–4:5). Jesus certainly seems to agree (Rev. 2:14–15, 20; 3:2, 15–17; 22:12).

Conclusions

To wrap up the various strands, what we've seen is that the biblical concept of "preaching Christ" means that:

1. Our evangelistic messages must align with Luke 24:45–47, and not be presented in showman-like fashion,
2. When an aspect of an OT CUT's message is Old Covenant-specific, we should update it to reflect its New Covenant equivalent,
3. We preach Christ not only when we preach Jesus' person or work, but also when we preach New Covenant theology or ethics.

How Can We Seamlessly Move to Christ?

While the biblical requirements for preaching Christ from the OT are generally met by preaching the THT instead of its OTM, there are still good reasons to use other ways to move to Christ in the sermon. Done well, moving to Christ can enrich listeners' faith and appeal to their emotions effectively. It can be powerful when listeners understand and feel a connection with the plan to redeem the world that God announced understatedly in Genesis 3:15. It's also powerful when people feel a connection to Jesus Christ. Christians are Christ-followers, and it can be a delightful twist in the sermon when we are reminded of his centrality.

Two Criteria for Seamlessly Moving to Christ
Any moves to Christ must be seamless to be effective. They must arise organically, at natural places in the sermon. They must not take over the sermon or encumber it as we preach through the CUT and communicate its message. They must support the text, its message, and the unity of the sermon.

Two criteria guide any moves to Christ. First, we must not misinterpret the text. The dictum, "*a text cannot mean what it never could have meant to its author or* [original] *readers*"[9] applies to the original meaning of every biblical text and also to our moves to Christ. Agreeing with Stuart, we must not spiritualize or allegorize CUTs by suggesting their details symbolically represent or prefigure "truths" about Christ. We must not "over-typologize" by making speculative statements about how a character foreshadows Jesus Christ. For example, it would be a mistake to say things like, "Joshua has the same name as Jesus; as a conqueror he points to The Conqueror," or "Ezra came to his people from afar; entered into Jerusalem on a donkey; prayed before crises; taught what was to many a new law; and purified the nation, and so on. His life points directly to the Savior."[10]

It would also be a mistake to accidentally misinterpret the text by indicating, either verbally or in bulletin notes, that a move to

---

9. Fee and Stuart, *How to Read the Bible for All Its Worth*, 77.
10. Stuart, *Old Testament Exegesis*, 183. See also Fee and Stuart, *How to Read the Bible for All Its Worth*, 107–10.

Christ is a main point or subpoint, even though in an academic outline of the sermon it would be a subpoint. This is because when listeners think of "point," they think of a prescriptive idea that's taught in (a specific portion of) the text.

Second, moves to Christ must complement the sermon. While sermons may contain more than one move to Christ, they must arise at appropriate places and not disrupt the sermon's flow or unity. This means that informal moves to Christ won't occur as we preach through the text. It also means that formal, pre-conclusion moves should take no longer than three minutes because longer ones would hinder the communication of the THT, disrupt the unity of the sermon, and push out concrete application, which is an implicit form of preaching Christ.

Informal Moves to Christ

Informal moves to Christ occur when we seamlessly but legitimately integrate Jesus Christ, the gospel, or the overarching plan of God into a part of the sermon that's not dedicated specifically for that purpose. For example, sometimes it can occur in our restatements of the question in the Focus, or as we Set the Stage.

A great place to make an informal move to Christ is in the transition to the application section. Having preached through a text written under the Old Covenant, it can be effective in that transition to mention how we live under a different covenant because of Jesus Christ. This connects the audience and message to Christ and also helps listeners incorporate further the biblical metanarrative into their own worldview, which is something contemporary listeners need.

> [Transition to Application section] We live at a different stage in God's plans. It's no longer God's central concern to fill the earth. At seven billion people, that requirement has been fulfilled. That was an early stage.

> God went on. He established a covenant with Abraham. Through Abraham came the nation Israel. From Israel was born Jesus Christ, who lived the perfect life in our place, died on the cross for our sins, and rose again from the dead.
>
> In our context, what can we do now that we've seen that God's redemptive plans will prevail?

Formal (Pre-Conclusion) Move to Christ

Should we decide to make a formal move to Christ, the best place to do it is just prior to entering the conclusion. By this point, we've preached through the CUT and applied the THT. Instead of going immediately to the conclusion, we could take a moment to remind listeners of the centrality of Jesus Christ. What follows are a number of good ways to do that, although we ought not assume that any of these options is the best choice, or even a legitimate one, for every CUT.

Ask How/Why Christ Makes the THT Possible

One potentially excellent option is to ask "how" or "why" Christ makes the THT possible. Here's how we could make such a move for the THT, "God will use us to fulfill his plan of salvation, but sin brings discipline":

> **[MOVE TO CHRIST]** But why can God use us in spite of our sin? Because of Jesus Christ. No matter how much repenting we do. No matter how much we plead for forgiveness, if it wasn't for Jesus Christ, his death on the cross for our sins, his perfect life in our place, his resurrection from the dead, God couldn't forgive us. We couldn't be God's ambassadors. God couldn't use us to fulfill his plan of salvation. Without Jesus Christ, we would all be lost. Let's be sure to worship him with our whole heart, the entirety of our being.

Show How the Text Reminds Us of the Need for Christ

Another potentially excellent option is to show how the CUT reminds us of the *need* for Jesus Christ. This is different than typology, which shows how the CUT foreshadows Jesus Christ. For the same sermon from 2 Samuel 11–12, here's how we could make such a move to Christ:

> **[MOVE TO CHRIST]** Our passage this morning reminds us of the need for Jesus Christ. God has been working his plan of salvation since the Fall. Every step of the way he runs into a problem: humans, us. When King David arrived on the scene, Israel was hopeful; David was faithful. But he too sinned, and sinned grievously.
>
> Our passage reminds us of the *need* for a faithful king, one who would rule God's people in righteousness and truth. Friends, our passage reminds us of the *need* for Jesus Christ. Without him, without the perfections of his holiness, God's people—past and future—could never experience the full blessings of God, neither in this life nor the next. It's only through him that the blessings of God are Yes and Yes. Entrust yourself to him . . . fully . . . today.

Christiconic

Another potentially excellent option is to share how Christ is the perfect image of what it means to put the THT into practice: "This is the crux of christiconic interpretation: in that he [Jesus] perfectly fulfilled divine demand, every pericope [i.e., legitimate preaching text] of Scripture implicitly portrays a facet of the image . . . of Christ."[11] Although christiconic interpretation is not really about how to make a formal move to Christ in the sermon, it can be appropriated that way:

---

11. Kuruvilla, *Privilege the Text!*, 232.

> [MOVE TO CHRIST] In calling us to align ourselves with God's redemptive plans, God is calling us to Christlikeness. It is Christ alone who aligns himself perfectly with God's redemptive plans. It is Christ alone who endured the trials and tribulations of human life perfectly.
>
> When we align ourselves with God's redemptive plans, we align ourselves with Jesus Christ. When we trust in Jesus Christ, our failures are hidden in Christ, and Christ's righteousness is ours. The more fully we align ourselves with God's redemptive plans, the more our life reflects Jesus Christ. He alone is worthy of all praise, glory, and honor.

Greidanus' Seven Ways

Sidney Greidanus has devoted significant time and effort to discerning ways that we can move to Christ legitimately in sermons from the OT. He identifies seven ways, although he notes that not all of them can be used for every passage.

Some of his ways, such as redemptive-historical progression, analogy, or contrast, have their greatest potential as informal moves to Christ. Three of his ways, promise-fulfillment, NT references, and typology, can be effective as formal, pre-conclusion moves to Christ. However, for practical reasons, I recommend you avoid his longitudinal themes. It's hard to use this way to preach Christ in less than three minutes, so using it would almost certainly hinder the unity of the sermon and the communication of the THT. Greidanus has his own reservations about it: "In sermons one must handle longitudinal themes with care, for tracing a theme in detail can soon become tedious for the congregation."[12]

Since Greidanus has written extensively on the seven ways in *Preaching Christ from the Old Testament*, and exemplified them

---

12. Greidanus, *Preaching Christ from Daniel*, 42.

amply in *Preaching Christ from Genesis* and *Preaching Christ from Daniel*, there's no need to summarize his work here. We would all do well to read all of Greidanus' books, and benefit from his ways to move to Christ in the sermon.

CHAPTER 12

Finishing Well in the Conclusion

An excellent sermon is a coherent whole. It unifies around a central idea and progresses clearly from the opening words to the final thoughts. A conclusion gives the sermon a sense of completeness. Whereas the introduction prepares listeners for the text and its message and the body proclaims and applies them, the conclusion brings it all to a satisfying end.

Conclusions need not be long. We've already said what we need to say. We will surely deflate an otherwise excellent sermon if we spend ten minutes rehashing the message or sharing long stories, poems, or new ideas. All we need to do in the remaining moments is leave a lasting impression that encourages and exhorts listeners to put the THT into practice.

Elements of a Conclusion

Excellent conclusions typically contain three elements, usually in this order: Review, Final Push, and Closing Affirmation.

Review

We should begin the conclusion with a review of the THT.[1] Be sure to state it, and then restate it immediately. We need to signal our entry into the conclusion by changing our cadence and using lower-key words like "Friends, today we've seen," or "So, this morning, we've seen," to sign-post the THT. However, avoid phrases like "In conclusion" or "Finally," as they sound stiff and draw too much attention to the inner workings of the sermon.

Remember to review the THT by stating it the way we've stated it throughout the sermon. We'll confuse listeners at the last moment by stating it in a way they've never heard. Does this mean we can't state the THT in a fresh way? No, we can do that, if we want to. However, it needs to be a restatement—not the first time it's said.

> [REVIEW] And so, friends, What is God doing with your life? My life? This morning we've seen that God is doing whatever he sees fit. [restate:] God's taking us on a journey to accomplish his purposes.

Final Push

After the Review, make a Final Push that urges listeners to put the THT into practice. There are many ways to do this. We could share an inspiring illustration and follow it with an exhortation. We could provide a compact PPA. Tie-back closes—where we return to something we said or did in the Engage—can be particularly effective because, more than any other close, listeners experience the sense that the sermon has come full circle. Whatever form the Final Push takes, keep it brief, remain positive, and include a call to action.

---

1. If we wanted to get technical, we could make the case that the Review is the last piece of the sermon body. If this was a book on preaching the Epistles, I would make that case for pedagogical reasons. Regardless, listeners hear the Review as if it's the start of the conclusion.

> [FINAL PUSH] We can make plans—and we should. But whatever direction God ultimately takes us, we must trust him.
>
> Maybe your life's a bit like Joseph's. God's taken you on a number of twists and turns you never saw coming. You may feel, "God, I don't like this. I didn't sign up for this. Lord, I need some relief."
>
> Whatever your circumstances, know this: God has a plan and a purpose for your life—even if he never tells you what it is. You play an integral role in some aspect of God's kingdom. Embrace it. Trust God. Persevere.

Closing Affirmation

If an excellent introduction opens the heart, and an excellent sermon body deposits the text and its message into the heart, then it may be said that an excellent conclusion secures the text and its message in the heart. In order to sew up God's Word in the heart, it can be helpful to express to listeners our joy-filled confidence that they desire to serve the Lord, or that they will trust God by putting the THT into practice.

There is no single way to do this, and if you're a wordsmith, take advantage of it. A simple sentence, delivered with a gentle, warm smile, like, "I trust you will" can work. So can a more developed affirmation:

> [CLOSING AFFIRMATION] Friends, God is at work in us. He is working in your life, to fulfill his purposes. When I look across this room, I see the hand of God working to save the world. It's a wild adventure, but God says, "Hold on. Trust me." I trust you will.

Some pastors find this difficult. A little jaded, their experience tells them many listeners are not particularly interested in putting biblical truth into practice. To ask them to express confidence in their congregation may feel like lying. We return to Augustine:

> The secret of his [Augustine's] success is that he makes allies of his congregations, identifying himself with them and addressing them as "we" and "holy brethren." He is realistic about their limitations but he never belittles them, remembering that Christ is at work among them. . . . He is both a towering theologian and a sensitive pastor.[2]

We also need to remember that spiritual growth usually requires a supportive catalyst, someone who envisions progress in spite of present appearances. Parents recognize this. We must endear ourselves to our children; we must make a positive, emotional investment in them, even as they defy us daily. Likewise, if we proclaim God's Word without any confidence that listeners will follow it, our nonverbal cues will give us away, and the likelihood they'll put the THT into practice will be reduced. Even Paul, after rebuking the Galatians, could say, "I have confidence in the Lord that you will take no other view [than mine]" (5:10).

Mistakes to Avoid

Conclusions don't have to be perfect to be effective. Nonetheless, there are three common mistakes to avoid. First, do not put the sermon's main application in the conclusion. The role of the conclusion is to wrap up the message. It's not the place to throw in application that we neglected to include earlier.

Second, avoid introspective questions. Questions like, "Do you trust in God when things get difficult?" or "How often do you follow God when money's tight?" are counterproductive. Listeners rarely respond to them, and when they do, it may be to judge others: "I don't think Avery and Taylor do. I hope they're listening."

---

2. Dunn-Wilson, *A Mirror for the Church*, 93, 98.

Finishing Well in the Conclusion

You want to leave the sermon on a positive, affirming note, where listeners leave inspired to live out the THT. Introspective questions are incompatible with that aim.

Third, avoid anything long: quotes, poems, songs, etc. Concluding is like landing a plane. When we reach our destination, we need to touch down, not circle the airport needlessly.

CHAPTER 13

From Good to Excellent

Following the recommendations of the previous chapters will yield consistently good sermons from OT narratives. Following also the recommendations in this chapter can produce consistently excellent sermons.

Pray

Prayer is a dynamic act that works much like preaching. Both are human actions that the Spirit uses to bring about God's plans and purposes (Eph. 3:14–16; 2 Tim. 3:16–4:5). Although no formula for preaching or prayer can guarantee the results we desire, it's still important to be diligent at both. Of his preaching ministry, Paul writes, "I worked harder than any of them, though it was not I, but the grace of God that is with me" (1 Cor. 15:10b). As for prayer, he urges, "Continue steadfastly in prayer, being watchful in it with thanksgiving" (Col. 4:2).

Prayer, then, is a priority. Reflecting on God's call for us to rely on his strength in our preaching and service, John Piper developed the acronym APTAT as a guide to prayer. He uses it during the church service, but there's no reason we can't use most of it throughout sermon preparation:

1. **A**dmit to the Lord that without him we can do nothing.
2. **P**ray for help to deliver a faithful and effective message.
3. **T**rust in a specific promise of God.
4. **A**ct wisely, knowing God will work through us.
5. **T**hank God after the sermon for empowering us to, at least in some measure, preach his Word by the Spirit's power.[1]

Dedicate Fifteen Focused Hours to Sermon Preparation

Not enough time, or distracted time, can keep us from developing sermons that are accurate, relevant, clear, and inspiring. It takes about fifteen hours over three or four days for most of us to develop an excellent sermon, and most of that time is not spent studying the text. It's spent developing the introduction, crafting the movements, and creating concrete application.

Most pastors today develop one sermon a week, which makes fifteen hours possible for the committed and efficient preacher. If you preach more than one sermon a week—or, in the case of one South Korean pastor I know, fourteen—this may not be possible. It's important, however, to minimize distractions during that time. We miss the full value of these fifteen hours if we use some of that time to check email, call parishioners, talk to folks in the hallway, or post messages on social media sites. Sunukjian notes that excellent preaching

> is the hardest and best thing we will ever do. *It's the hardest, for it will take the most rigorous mental ability and discipline God has given us.* We will find ourselves tempted to do anything but the hard study required—we'll schedule meetings, arrange counseling appointments, tackle administrative tasks, clean our fingernails, find a sermon on the internet, or settle for some superficial approach to our passage—anything to

---

1. Adapted from Piper, *The Supremacy of God in Preaching*, 46–49.

> avoid the sheer labor required. . . . *It's the hardest thing we will ever do, but it's . . . the best thing we can do for our ministries, and it's the best thing we can do for our own personal lives.*"[2]

That excellent preaching requires focused sermon preparation means that it shouldn't surprise us that the best preachers are typically introverts. Abraham Kuruvilla, a leading homiletician, interviews top preachers frequently for his blog, Homiletix (http://www.homiletix.com). At last check, seventy percent of those he's asked self-identified as introverts, eighteen percent as mixed or unknown (which probably indicates they too are introverts), and twelve percent as extroverts. With less of an inclination to be social, it's often easier for introverts to use their time more efficiently in sermon preparation, should they desire.

Yet I know an extroverted preacher who manages to spend the necessary time, despite being easily distracted. He goes to a separate office (or coffee shop when traveling) with food and a timed lockbox called The Kitchen Safe. He throws his keys, wallet, and phone in it, then programs the safe to remain locked for a set period of time. He uses software to block access to files, programs, and websites that distract him. He makes it so that the only thing he can do during sermon preparation is work on the sermon. He says that when all distractions are eliminated, it's somehow easy for him to remain focused, all day if necessary.

Use Humor

Humor is anything we do that lightens the mood of the audience. It can be a powerful tool in any preacher's toolbox. It's used most effectively in the introduction, before poignant moments, or shortly after the halfway point in the sermon. Humor need not take the form of a joke, which might be good for us to know, if we struggle to remember or deliver them well! Preachers who refrain from humor tend to do

---

2. Sunukjian, *Invitation to Biblical Preaching*, 15 (emphasis added).

so for two reasons: (1) their favorite dynamic preachers, whose dynamism affords them the luxury of neglecting humor, advise against it; and (2) they are unable to relax in the pulpit.

Preaching "invites—even demands—the use of humor."[3] It has tremendous potential for identification, for it "is a powerful way for humans to establish and signal connection with each other."[4] Humor can be a catalyst for change because it lowers listeners' defenses. For example, preachers can use it to relax the audience in the moments leading up to a profound or poignant statement, making it easier for that truth to reach their hearts. It can also reinvigorate the sermon. Listening takes effort. Using humor (or other attention regaining strategy) halfway through the sermon can make the second half just as easy to listen to as the first.

Our ability to use humor depends on our ability to relax *in the pulpit*. Those of us who are driven, controlling, idealistic, or perfectionistic commonly find humor difficult. Yet the safer we feel *in the pulpit* and the more we are fully present and delighted to be with the audience, the easier it is for humor to flow out of us, both in sermon preparation and in the pulpit.

The primary characteristic of good, clean, healing humor is silliness. Here are ten ways we can refresh listeners with humor:

1. Poke fun at ourselves.
2. End a story or joke in an unexpected way.
3. Juxtapose two things that don't normally go together.
4. Develop an idea with a cute story that involves kids.
5. Develop an idea with an amusing quip, quote, or definition.
6. Retell or restate a story or idea in an absurd way.
7. Draw out the humor in something with an absurd analogy.
8. Ask listeners a silly question.
9. Ask listeners to discuss a lighthearted question.
10. Make an exaggerated facial expression or body movement.

---

3. Hooke, "Humor in Preaching," 187.
4. Ibid.

Humor has risks. It can make us the object of attention. Frederick Buechner writes, "If you are any good at all with words . . . you have to be so careful not to make it just a performance."[5] Arbitrarily invoked humor can detract from the message: "Certainly humor can be misused in sermons, as when the preacher begins with a joke that bears no relationship to the rest of the sermon."[6] It can also backfire, if the audience considers it inappropriate (cf. Eph. 4:29; 5:4).

We must also avoid humor that projects a sense of superiority. Biblically, it's hard to justify pulpit humor that makes others out to be less intelligent, sophisticated, or faithful. Although such humor does occur in the Bible—for example, God laughs at the nations in Psalm 2:4; Elijah taunts the prophets of Baal in 1 Kings 18:27–28; Paul's sarcasm drips in Galatians 5:12 against those who advocate for the spiritual necessity of circumcision; and Paul mocks the "super-apostles" in 2 Corinthians 11:5 (although he laments having to do so in 12:11)—the circumstances of its use are *not* sufficiently parallel to warrant its use in the sermon.

Therefore, use humor, but use it to refresh and unite, not divide. Refrain from anything that would incline us to give even a lighthearted apology or require us to say, "I'm joking. I'm joking!"

Add a Little Creativity

A little creativity goes a long way. It increases interest and communicates subtly to the audience our willingness to serve their listening needs. However, excessive displays of creativity or outright showmanship cause listeners to take the preacher and the message less seriously. We listen to those who serve us; we are entertained by those who wow us.

As we look to add a little creativity, we must not try to be more creative than our tech people can handle. Better to train them or

---

5. Quoted in Shore, "Leave Them Wanting More," 125.
6. Hooke, 187.

depend on low-tech methods than to sidetrack the sermon. Clumsy or failed attempts to incorporate technology project incompetence.

Enhance the Multi-Sensory Appeal

That multi-sensory experiences are valuable can be seen in OT practices like animal sacrifice, and NT ones like communion and baptism. It can also be seen in the way Jesus preached. He would often do things like travel to a religiously significant spot, climb in a boat, hop on a donkey, or enter the home of an outcast before teaching. While he taught, he also did things like draw on the ground or spit. And certainly his death and resurrection appearances are multi-sensory experiences!

Live, in-person sermons have tremendous potential to break down emotional barriers and stimulate transformation by means of appeals that make use of visual, auditory, and tactile elements. A classic example of multi-sensory appeal—but one that is disappearing rapidly, and not because of technology—occurs when listeners hold a physical Bible in their hands and see for themselves that what the preacher is saying is taught in the text.

Old Testament narratives are full of rich images we can incorporate into our sermons. For example, noticing that Genesis 11:1–9 mentions brick and mortar, we could find a low-tech way to incorporate those materials into the sermon. In 2 Samuel 11–12, King David is a main character. Since kings are known for wearing crowns, we could find a way to incorporate a crown into the sermon. We could use a crown as a symbol of self-rule in one part of the sermon and as a symbol of God's rule in another. When preaching Genesis 2:4–3:24, we could play an audio clip of the "Happy Days" theme song to help convey Adam's joy at seeing Eve. Adding these kinds of low-tech touches once every three to four weeks can meaningfully enhance our preaching.

A word of caution on the use of audio and video clips: There needs to be a compelling reason to use a clip longer than thirty seconds. These media engross listeners quickly, and when that happens listeners lose track of the sermon and their connection with us.

Further, listeners rarely get what we want them to get out of longer clips, so their use tends to be counterproductive—having a form of relevance but lacking its power.

An oft-neglected key to using physical objects is to avoid walking to the platform with them; it looks goofy and amateurish. They should be on stage already. Before the service, find a place where they can both blend in until they are needed and be retrieved seamlessly during the sermon. Place your items there before the service, or if necessary have someone on the worship team move them inconspicuously to that spot before the sermon begins. Further, don't draw attention to them before you're ready to use them.

Preach a First Person Narrative Sermon Occasionally
Preach a first person narrative sermon one to three times per year. In this sermon form, preachers proclaim their CUTs as if they are a character in the narrative. Most congregations love this sermon form, so long as it's not used too often.

There are a number of books to help you use this sermon form, but know that they tend to endorse the Universalizing the Plot Line Approach (see chapter 1). Therefore, use them to help you deliver the sermon, after you've arrived at the THT.

Deliver the Message Smoothly

No sermon is excellent without a fluent delivery. All preachers—especially those with less than five years of full-time preaching experience—need to keep an eagle eye on their delivery skills. Remember, listeners are untrained in biblical hermeneutics, so our delivery skills are the primary way they assess our credibility. Our delivery is smooth when our words flow out of us effortlessly, with good eye contact, natural gestures, and vocal variety. A smooth delivery also incorporates technology seamlessly, as if it is an extension of ourselves.

Excellent delivery is mostly a head game. We must feel safe—very safe—in the pulpit. We must be delighted to be there, feeling as if there is nowhere else we'd rather be at that moment than giving that message to that audience. We must delight in the audience and be convinced the audience likes us and wants us to succeed. We must not worry about stumbling over words or losing our place. For preachers with the best delivery skills, the pulpit is the safest place on earth. Fear, anxiety, and related eccentricities may keep them from holding ordinary conversations with members of the congregation, but when they walk into the pulpit they are at ease. The best "them" comes out.

Some signs of pulpit insecurity are obvious. Filler words like "uh," "like," "right?" "to be honest with you," and "you know?" have no place in the sermon, and we risk losing the confidence of listeners who don't know us well or aren't convinced of our preaching abilities if we use them. Research indicates that filler words can have a significant negative impact on perceptions of our credibility.[7]

Some signs are less obvious. We may be unaware of our own nervous miscues like fidgeting with the microphone, adjusting our glasses, or touching our noses or hair. We might put our hands together in front of us or hold onto the pulpit as our resting position, instead of letting them hang comfortably to the side. We may have never thought twice about our penchant for using rigid or chopping arm gestures, or noticed that our gestures always involve both arms.

While not all miscues are avoidable, it's important to not exacerbate the problem by drawing attention to them. When we stumble over a word or say something that doesn't come out right, we need to ignore it and move on. If the "slide guy" doesn't follow our instructions, don't draw further attention to it. Unless there is a compelling reason, ignore miscues and move forward. We highlight our own or our church's incompetence when we don't.

Maintain a Disciplined Tongue

A disciplined tongue represents God faithfully and winsomely. It neither soft-pedals God's Word, distorts its message, nor hinders

---

7. Sunukjian, "Credibility of the Preacher," 258–59.

its reception. With the first assumed, the focus here is on the latter two. Excellent preachers do not sacrifice long-term health for short-term growth. Shallow, simplistic, or colorful preaching, if done with skill, can produce a large following among the easily or already convinced—and needlessly turn off many others. Preaching with a disciplined tongue supports our desire to reach a wider cross-section of people with credibility. We need to take a both/and approach, where we encourage those who trust us, win those on the cusp of conversion, *and* reach holdouts who need a faith that's reasonable. We can do that if we are real, winsome, and careful with self-disclosure.

Be Real

One effect of living in a pluralistic society is that listeners are influenced by people from a variety of cultures and worldviews. Many of them are at least mildly open to placing their faith in Christ. I'm thinking especially about teenagers, young adults, and those with analytical minds. However, their life experiences don't always match up with what the Bible teaches.

Actually, their difficulty is often not with what the Bible teaches—it's with what *we* teach. The problem is, they don't know the difference. I talk to people regularly who are suspicious of the simplistic, all-encompassing solutions to life's problems that they hear from preachers. When preachers indicate that the right quality and quantity of prayer, Bible reading, or accountability is the cure for all personal sin, they're skeptical, especially if they've had family or friends experience abuse, divorce, or addiction. They find it hard to believe any sensible person can believe the earth or universe is thousands of years old. They're dubious when Christians claim that God speaks to them in a semi-revelatory manner on a regular basis.[8]

---

8. See Garry Friesen and J. Robin Maxson, *Decision Making and the Will of God*; Haddon W. Robinson, *Decision-Making by the Book*; Bruce K. Waltke, *Finding the Will of God: A Pagan Notion?*.

We can eliminate much of this problem by taking an extra moment during sermon preparation to consider our word choice. We often accidentally use words that contradict our considered opinion. For example, preachers frequently use "will" in sentences when, if they thought about it, they would most certainly say "may" or "might," or leave out the statement entirely. Likewise, preachers commonly, but accidentally, speak about God or the Christian life as if they can be reduced to magical formulas, solutions, or biblical models. When I ask preachers, "Do you really believe . . ." and follow that with something they said, their reply is invariably akin to "Oh, well no, not exactly." They then follow that with something that's usually reasonable. As for why they said it, they generally share that it sounded good when they came up with it and didn't think twice about it.

There's another problem with careless imprecisions: Many Christians buy into them and use them to build neat fences. These fences produce artificial criteria by which they can measure their own lives and the lives of others. For some, these fences seem to work. For others, their life or faith crumbles when their fences break, or they experience heartache when their kids leave the faith, because they equate the faith with the simplistic views of their well-meaning parents.

Be Winsome

Preaching that's winsome is emotionally and intellectually respectful. Most of us know enough to avoid overly casual language. For example, references to sex, private parts, or bad words, even if made euphemistically, typically and unnecessarily hurt our credibility in the eyes of some. Just because our friends don't mind such language at lunch doesn't mean the congregation appreciates it on Sunday.

Winsome preaching strikes a balance in the presentation of ideas, being neither emotionally charged nor intellectually distant. We need to avoid over-the-top rhetoric. For example, comparing any person or group to Hitler or the Nazis is uncalled for, regardless of whether we feel the analogy is legitimate. A friend once heard his pastor describe how to skin an animal. Such wild analogies or illustrations hurt more than help. The saying "when in doubt, leave it out" applies here.

We need to present differing viewpoints fairly. Preaching should not resemble demagoguery. Making another's views seem easily refutable because we've distorted them is not acceptable for a freshman public speaking student, and it's not acceptable in the pulpit.

We need to present opposing viewpoints in a way that a thoughtful proponent would consider fair. However, this does not mean we ought to provide a thorough account of the view; indeed, we should not. Research indicates that overwhelming an audience with the arguments of an opposing view causes the audience to doubt the speaker's own view, even after the speaker refutes it. Nonetheless, it's fine to call out a view for what it is. If it's dangerous, make your case. If it's unbiblical, say so. Just avoid exaggerated claims or outlandish statements.

Be Careful with Self-Disclosure

Self-disclosure refers to anything we say or do that reveals our private "feelings, values, and/or personal experiences"[9]—our inner world. One benefit of self-disclosure is identification, for we show ourselves to be an "everyman." For example, I once shared in a sermon the three requests I make of my children before taking them on a long drive: Go to the bathroom now; keep your hands to yourselves; and don't ask more than five times, "How long until we get there?"

Self-disclosure is also potentially damaging. If we're not careful, allowing listeners into our inner world can deepen the alienation gap. Just as it's inappropriate to burden someone we don't know well with our personal problems, it's inappropriate to share information that's best reserved for a spouse, mentor, or therapist. Jeffrey Arthurs writes, "Preachers should count the cost not only for themselves but also for their congregations. An expositor's purpose is not to burden people with emotional baggage."[10]

---

9. Arthurs and Gurevich, "Theological and Rhetorical Perspectives on Self-disclosure in Preaching," 215.
10. Ibid., 223.

But what if it's a sin we've already overcome—can we share it? Not always and not immediately. For victories over serious problems like family strife, anger, addiction, or lying, wisdom dictates that we wait twenty years, unless the problem was overcome before the age of twenty-one or shortly after our conversion or public backsliding. Anything other than that will likely "create awkwardness and distrust rather than a sense of intimacy and trust."[11]

We don't need to wait as long to share mild, everyday failures. It can be okay, for example, to illustrate an idea by sharing about a mellow argument with a family member (provided we get their permission), but *we must be certain listeners will perceive it as minor!* Even for minor conflicts, we should only share those where we are the primary or only guilty party. Not only is it unhelpful to use the pulpit to shed negative light on other people—listeners do not appreciate it. It would be better to remove any identifiable information and turn the conflict into a PPA.

Sharing foibles unwisely is not the only risk of self-disclosure. We need to be careful to not present ourselves as models of virtue. Listeners secretly resent preachers who give the impression they're near-perfect, or smarter than everyone else. Use caution, but it's best to share more examples of our failures than our successes.

We also need to refrain from revealing any of our socially unacceptable eccentricities, idiosyncrasies, or peculiar values. In personal conversations, pastors have shared with me how they're taking their wife's miscarriage in stride, opined that having more than two kids is a burden, whined about pastoral visitation, and expressed outrage about issues that are quite unspectacular. Disclosing things like these in the pulpit can produce a degree of alienation in listeners that lasts months or even years.

Part of the difficulty with self-disclosure is that we are often unaware of all the ways we are profoundly different than our listeners. What we feel is common or reasonable might seem bizarre to them. Before we self-disclose, we should consider running it by

---

11. Ibid., 224.

our spouse or a good friend. As a rule of thumb, if we're tempted to preface it with something like "I know it's a little different" or "I know it's a little unusual," it's probably best to leave it out.

Write a Manuscript, Then Ditch It

Developing a manuscript is one of the best things a skilled preacher can do. We can't wing accurate interpretation, concrete application, or clear structure. Each takes careful thought to develop. Manuscripts enable us to review the sermon and notice weak spots. For example, it can be easy to neglect to remind listeners of the Focus with our movements (see guideline 2 of chapter 6). Reviewing the manuscript can fix that serious defect.

Notice how the sermon manuscripts in the back of this book label each section and indent subordinate sections. I didn't do that only for your benefit; that's how I write my sermons. It adds only five to ten minutes to sermon preparation and helps me review my sermons more effectively. At first glance, my students find it intimidating; but once they start to do it, it relieves them of stress.

So write a manuscript—but then ditch it. Excellent preaching inspires, and inspiring preaching requires a heart-to-heart connection. It involves one soul reaching another with a message about God, his world, his will, and the relationship he wants us to have with him and one another. The more we rely on our notes, the more the sermon becomes an informational transaction, a lecture.

Does that mean we should preach without notes? Ideally, yes, but we don't live in an ideal world. I don't let my students preach with any notes because it surprises them to learn they can do it. Furthermore—as I've learned with my public-speaking students—if I let them use their notes, most will rely on them.

For pastors, I recommend using whatever amount of notes maximizes a smooth delivery. The reality is some of us worry we'll lose our place and embarrass ourselves, and when we preach without any notes, listeners sense our unease, our internal scramble for words, as we focus more on getting that next sentence out than reaching listeners' hearts.

For some of us, this means bringing up the entire manuscript and almost never looking at it; the manuscript functions like a security blanket. It calms the nerves enough to keep us from stumbling over our words. Others of us may find that a one-page outline is sufficient.

I don't blame you if you're not yet ready to embrace preaching without your notes. However, begin the transition. Take steps each week to simultaneously relax and to reduce your dependence on notes. After each sermon, assess your nerves, the smoothness of your delivery, and your ability to delight in the audience. Make adjustments, and repeat. Remember, the goal is internalize the sermon, not memorize it. You can do it with an orally clear sermon and a little effort.

Practice the Sermon

Our sermons are, without question, better if we take an hour to practice them a day or two early. Those of us who preach at multiple weekend services understand this, as the second or third sermon is often the best. Practice is particularly useful for developing our delivery skills.

Practicing is also beneficial to those with excellent delivery skills who want to better integrate hermeneutics and oral clarity into their preaching. It can be easier to deliver inspiring messages, if we never question our handling of the text or oral clarity. I worked with a student once who had incredible delivery skills, but handled the text poorly, despite the impressive number of exegesis courses he'd taken. It hurt his feelings to hear this after his first in-class sermon. He made one attempt to improve, but with his confidence shaken, his delivery skills suffered. He admitted that if the congregation was happy with his preaching, that was good enough for him.

Practice relaxes us. It helps us internalize the message. It enables us to preach on Sunday with little or no notes. It can empower us to move out from behind the pulpit and connect more deeply with listeners by means of improved eye contact, gestures, energy, and sense of friendliness.

Practice in the sanctuary, if possible. Take one hour to run through the sermon. Think through your gestures, as well as where you'll stand at various points in the sermon. Since the audience faces us, remember to gesture in the opposite direction. For example, our arms need to move from right-to-left to indicate progress.

Don't worry if the sermon doesn't seem very good in practice. Practice tends to feel that way because of its artificial nature. Somehow, however, it makes a good sermon even better.

Get a Preaching Coach

Few things can enhance our preaching quicker than a good preaching coach. The closest thing most of us get to one is our college or seminary preaching professors. I've taken more than ten preaching courses, and I'm indebted to my professors. Homileticians who know their stuff are worth their weight in gold.

Good books on preaching can also transform our preaching. They are ready resources, able to serve us at a moment's notice. They provide new insight and convey time-tested concepts in fresh ways.

What makes good preaching coaches so effective is their ability to provide a keen second set of eyes on a consistent basis. They can identify issues we can't see in ourselves. They can work with us closely to master skills we can't seem to develop. They can provide guidance on the handling of texts that are difficult to preach with excellence. They can note our progress and do it every time we preach. And since they help you with sermons you're already doing for church, the extra time commitment is minimal.

Here are three ways to find a preaching coach. First, you could pursue a Doctor of Ministry degree in preaching, and see if one of your professors will coach you outside of class at an agreed-upon rate. That's what I did, and I loved it. Second, you could use Gordon-Conwell Theological Seminary's Sermon DoctorRx (http://www.gordonconwell.edu). This is a popular choice. They listen to your sermons and provide feedback within a week. Third, you could use Preaching*Works* (http://www.preachingworks.com), the organization I lead. We have a variety of services and are able to discuss your or your staff's sermons before and after you deliver them by phone or video conference.

APPENDIX A

Organic Sermon Structure

The following outline provides the basic flow/order of sermons from OT narratives. In isolation, this outline is unlikely to make sense, but you may find it quite helpful as you read through or review the chapters in Part II.

Introduction (Ch. 5)

[ENGAGE] Gain interest related to the Focus.
[FOCUS] Raise a question the THT answers or state the THT.
[SET THE STAGE] Provide background information (if needed).
[PREVIEW] Preview the direction the sermon will take.
[ANNOUNCE THE PASSAGE] Announce the book and chapter.

Preach Through The Text (Ch. 6–7)

[Transition] Provide a transition to the movement that follows (optional).
[MOVEMENT (or alternative)] Illuminate the verses about to be read.

[READ] Read only the verses this movement (or alternative) covers.
[EXPLAIN] Explain anything else that's necessary (usually omitted).

[Transition] Provide a transition to the movement that follows (optional).
[MOVEMENT (or alternative)] Illuminate the verses about to be read.

[READ] Read only the verses this movement (or alternative) covers.
[EXPLAIN] Explain anything else that's necessary (usually omitted).

[Follow the basic flow above until the text's been preached through.]

****Decide whether to state the THT after the text has been preached through, or in conjunction with one of your final movements (ch. 8).****

Develop the THT (Ch. 9–11)

[BUY] Raise and overcome objections to the THT (optional).
[APPLY] Apply the THT to listeners with PPAs.
[MOVE TO CHRIST] Make a legitimate move to Christ (if desired).

Conclusion (Ch. 12)

[REVIEW] Review the THT.
[FINAL PUSH] Urge listeners to put the THT into practice.
[CLOSING AFFIRMATION] Close with a brief encouraging word.

APPENDIX B

Sermon from 2 Samuel 11–12

This sermon was delivered to a congregation in Phoenix, AZ. I preached from the New International Version, which was chosen to enhance clarity, as it was the translation most in the audience were using. The indentation and labels are retained from the original manuscript.

The THT's wording is altered slightly from the way it's written earlier in the book. Words that appear in the THT, or the question it answers, are italicized throughout the manuscript, except when they appear in the Focus or when the THT is "officially" stated in the body of the sermon (see ch. 6).

INTRODUCTION
[ENGAGE] A few years ago, a friend of mine became a Foreign Service Officer. Foreign Service Officers work at American embassies all over the world.

The head of each embassy is called an *ambassador*. *Ambassadors* are the highest-ranking representatives of their governments in the countries they serve in. *Ambassadors* are granted the authority to speak in that country on behalf of the President—and by extension, the American people.

In a moment, turn to the person next to you. Take a guess as to how many *ambassadors* the US has to foreign countries right now.

Here are some clues: There are approximately 180 countries. We don't have *ambassadors* for some countries, like North Korea. Small countries may share an *ambassador*. Some *ambassador* positions are vacant. Okay, turn to the person next to you.

[watch and smile comfortably for about a minute as listeners chat among themselves]

Here's the answer: Right now, the US has 128 ambassadors to other countries. [Add a comment or two, based on the audience's reaction.]

[**transition to Focus**] In God's kingdom, in God's eyes, every person who places their faith in Jesus Christ is an *ambassador*, an *ambassador* of Jesus Christ. That's true whether we're seven or 107. It's true whether our marriage is great, we're recently divorced, or single.

Ambassadors of Jesus Christ are called to further God's *plan of salvation*. God's *plan* began in Genesis 3:15. It continued through Abraham. Israel. It continues through to Christ and the gospel today, and into eternity. God calls us as *ambassadors* to act and speak in ways that bring people into a relationship with Jesus Christ.

We want to be a part of what God is doing. We want God to *use us* to *further his plan*. We know that God wants to *use us*. When we look at our lives, we also know we struggle to follow God. We make mistakes. We get *sidetracked by our own plans*. We *sin*.

We wonder less: "Does God want to use me?" And more: "*Will God use me?*"

Sermon from 2 Samuel 11–12

[FOCUS] What kind of ambassador of Christ will God use to fulfill his plan of salvation? [restate:] Who among us does God use to further the gospel? This morning we're going to look at a time in King David's life that answers that question.

[SET THE STAGE] When David was alive, God had one primary *ambassador*: the king of Israel. The king was the primary instrument through which God *fulfilled* his purposes. Israel knew this and had a desire to know what kind of king, what kind of *ambassador*, God would use.

David was Israel's second king. Israel's first king was Saul. Saul was an *ambassador* too, but God stopped using Saul after he sinned—for what we might consider lesser crimes than those we'll soon discover David commits.

[PREVIEW] It's in the context of David's first failure as king that we discover *what kind of ambassador, indeed ambassadors of Christ today, God will use to fulfill his plan of salvation.*

[ANNOUNCE THE PASSAGE] To get the answer to that question, let's open our Bibles to the book of 2 Samuel. . . . It's in the Old Testament, between Joshua and Kings . . . page 258 in the Blue Bibles . . . 2 Samuel chapter 11 . . . 2 Samuel 11.

[MOVEMENT] As the story opens, King David sends his top commander, Joab, and Israel's military to fight the Ammonites. Operation Besiege Rabbah is successful. David, however, remains home—*sidetracked* with his own *plans* to attend to.

[READ] Read with me verse 1, "¹In the spring, at the time when kings go off to war, David sent Joab out with the king's men and the whole Israelite army. They destroyed the Ammonites and besieged Rabbah. But David remained in Jerusalem."

[Transition] King David's *plan* begins to take shape.

[MOVEMENT] He wakes from a late-afternoon siesta. He takes a stroll on the palace roof. He looks around the city. As he looks toward the direction of Uriah's house—make no mistake, he knows where Uriah lives—he sees Uriah's wife, Bathsheba, bathing on the roof. David sends a servant to confirm it's her. Confirmed. David's *plan* is a common one among ancient kings: Assert authority over a possible rival by sleeping with his wives.[1] David has Bathsheba brought to him. He sleeps with her. He sends her away. But there's one problem: She's pregnant.

> [READ] Let's pick it up at verse 2: "²One evening David got up from his bed and walked around on the roof of the palace. From the roof he saw a woman bathing. The woman was very beautiful, ³and David sent someone to find out about her. The man said, 'Isn't this Bathsheba, the daughter of Eliam and the wife of Uriah the Hittite?' ⁴Then David sent messengers to get her. She came to him, and he slept with her. (She had purified herself from her uncleanness.)"—that's a nice way to say she could get pregnant—"Then she went back home. ⁵The woman conceived and sent word to David, saying, 'I am pregnant.'"
>
> [EXPLAIN] David's behavior is a power play against Uriah. Since we normally think of David here as falling, as stumbling, into adultery, I want to point out two things. First,

---

1. To sleep with a (possible) rival's wives or concubines was to assert or secure your right to the throne. Notice later in 2 Samuel 16:20–22 that David's son Absalom did this himself, against David. Further, "it was a rule in the ancient East that the whole of [the former] king's harem became the personal property of his successor." ISBE "Abishag"; cf. 2 Sam. 12:7–8. It's no surprise, therefore, that Solomon reacts the way he does in 1 Kings 2:22–25 where Adonijah, David's son and Solomon's older half-brother, has Bathsheba ask Solomon to let David's "nurse" Abishag be his (i.e., Adonijah's) wife.

Sermon from 2 Samuel 11–12

King David has the highest roof in the city. It's unlikely this is the first time he's noticed a woman bathing. People lived in tiny homes with no plumbing. Second, notice in verses 3 and 4: King David didn't pursue the woman until he knew exactly who she was: Uriah's wife.

[Transition] With Bathsheba pregnant, our *ambassador*-king finds himself in an unexpected predicament. How can he possibly get out of it?

[MOVEMENT] Our worst fears are realized: King David resolves to murder Uriah through "legal means." His first strategy: entrapment. David calls Uriah back from battle. He hobnobs about the war. "Hey, Uriah, go enjoy some alone time with Bathsheba." Marital relations are strictly forbidden in wartime. If Uriah complies, he's liable to receive a death sentence. Uriah leaves, and David's plan looks successful, until we learn of Uriah's integrity. He sleeps not with his wife, but in the servants' quarters.

[READ] Look at verse 6, "⁶So David sent this word to Joab: 'Send me Uriah the Hittite.' And Joab sent him to David. ⁷When Uriah came to him, David asked him how Joab was, how the soldiers were and how the war was going. ⁸Then David said to Uriah, 'Go down to your house and'"— [coughing sound]—"'wash your feet.' So Uriah left the palace, and a gift from the king was sent after him. ⁹But Uriah slept at the entrance to the palace with all his master's servants and did not go down to his house."

[Transition] David's 0-for-1, but undeterred. He tries again to entrap Uriah, to murder him through "legal means."

[MOVEMENT] The next day King David schmoozes Uriah. "Uriah, you're crazy. You've come all this way. Why didn't you go see your wife?" Uriah responds in a way a military veteran in those days would appreciate: "Absolutely not. Our forces are out there living in tents, fighting for the LORD. I'd never do that." David replies: "Fair enough. Just make sure you enjoy yourself tonight. Let's hang out and have a good time tonight. I'll send you back tomorrow." Our *ambassador*-king and Uriah party away that night. But come bedtime, Uriah sleeps in the servants' quarters.

> [READ] Read with me verses 10–13, "¹⁰When David was told, 'Uriah did not go home,' he asked him, 'Haven't you just come from a distance? Why didn't you go home?' ¹¹Uriah said to David, 'The ark and Israel and Judah are staying in tents, and my master Joab and my lord's men are camped in the open fields. How could I go to my house to eat and drink and lie with my wife? As surely as you live, I will not do such a thing!' ¹²Then David said to him, 'Stay here one more day, and tomorrow I will send you back.' So Uriah remained in Jerusalem that day and the next. ¹³At David's invitation, he ate and drank with him, and David made him drunk. But in the evening Uriah went out to sleep on his mat among his master's servants; he did not go home."

[Transition] After Uriah proves to have more integrity when drunk than David has sober, David finds himself 0-for-2. He decides to use a different "legal means" to murder Uriah.

[SUMMARIZE-WITHOUT-READING] David sends Uriah back to the battlefield with a note. Uriah doesn't know it, but it's his own death warrant. In the note David instructs Joab, his top military commander, to put Uriah on the front lines and then pull his men back, ensuring Uriah's death. David's *plan* succeeds. Uriah's murdered "legally" [11:14–25].

[EXPLAIN-AS-YOU-READ] Verse 26 tells us, "²⁶When Uriah's wife heard that her husband was dead, she mourned for him." In that culture, you were expected to grieve publicly for a period of time. We can assume, like anyone who loses a loved one, she grieved much longer, privately. Verse 27: "²⁷After the time of mourning was over, David had her brought to his house, and she became his wife and bore him a son." David's cover-up is complete. His public image is intact. The public may have even seen David as a hero who saved a deceased military hero's wife from possible destitution.

Yet we're left to wonder, *"Is this the kind of ambassador God will use to fulfill his plans?* Someone who abuses his power, covers up his tracks, and gets away with it? Where is God in all this? God, despite the way things look, has seen what's happened. He's not happy. Look at the end of verse 27: "But the thing David had done displeased the Lord."

[SUMMARIZE-WITHOUT-READING] God dispatches Nathan the prophet to confront David. Nathan begins with a parable-in-disguise: "Hey David, I have a story for you. I want to get your thoughts on it. There are these two men. One is rich. The other poor. The rich man has everything. The poor man nothing. Nothing, but a little lamb. He loves that lamb. He treats it like family. One day, the rich man welcomes a visitor. However, the rich man doesn't want to feed the visitor from his own flock, so he steals the poor man's lamb. He cooks it and feeds it to the visitor. David, what do you make of that?" [12:1–6].

David's furious at the rich man. He curses and condemns him. The rich man's behavior is outrageous.

[EXPLAIN-AS-YOU-READ] Let's pick it up at chapter 12, verse 7: "⁷Then Nathan said to David, 'You are the man!'" You're the one I'm talking about.

[MOVEMENT] Nathan continues. "David, this is what God says to you: *You are my ambassador.* I made you king. I anointed you with the Spirit. In return, you spurned my grace. You despised my word. You murdered poor Uriah, and you made his wife your own.

[READ] Look at the second half of verse 7: "⁷This is what the Lord, the God of Israel, says: 'I anointed you king over Israel, and I delivered you from the hand of Saul. ⁸I gave your master's'"—that is, King Saul's—"'house to you, and King Saul's wives into your arms. I gave you the house of Israel and Judah. And if all this had been too little, I would have given you even more. ⁹Why did you despise the word of the Lord by doing what is evil in his eyes? You struck down Uriah the Hittite with the sword and took his wife to be your own. You killed him with the sword of the Ammonites.'"

[Transition] It's at this point we discover *what kind of ambassador, even an ambassador of Christ today, God will use to fulfill his plan of salvation. We discover who among us God will use to further the gospel.*

[THT] We discover God that will use any ambassador to fulfill his plan of salvation. He will use us to further the gospel, even if we've gotten sidetracked by sin, if we will repent—if we will but turn back to him. But keep in mind: Sin brings discipline.

[MOVEMENT] We see this as David responds with *repentance*, and Nathan assures him of God's forgiveness. But *discipline* remains.

[READ] Read with me verses 13 and 14: "¹³Then David said to Nathan, 'I have sinned against the Lord.' Nathan replied, 'The Lord has taken away your sin. You are not going to die. ¹⁴But'"—*discipline* remains—"'because by doing this you have made the enemies of the Lord show utter contempt, the son born to you will die.'"

[EXPLAIN] David did the one thing Israel's first king, King Saul, wouldn't do: *repent*. King Saul played lip service. He uttered something that looked like an apology. But David *repents*. David's contrite. He doesn't pass the buck. God forgives David, which implies *God will still use him*. But David can't escape God's *discipline*.

[SUMMARIZE-WITHOUT-READING] Soon God's *discipline* hits home. The child's born. David pleads with God, knowing it's possible God could relent.[2] On the seventh day, the child dies [12:15–23].

[MOVEMENT] And then, God surprises us. God goes beyond implying that *he will use* his *ambassador*, King David, to further his *plans*. He proves it. Solomon is born, the one who *fulfills* the next step in God's redemptive *plans*. Imagine ancient Israel's relief. They, like us, can have confidence *God will indeed use a sinful, sometimes wayward, ambassador like King David, to fulfill his plans*:

> [READ] Look with me at verses 24 and 25, "²⁴Then David comforted his wife Bathsheba, and he went to her and lay with her. She gave birth to a son, and they named him Solomon. The Lord loved him; ²⁵and because the Lord loved him, he sent word through Nathan the prophet to name him Jedidiah."

[SUMMARIZE-WITHOUT-READING] In the verses that follow, God demonstrates his willingness to *use us* again, as he empowers Israel to complete its victory over the Ammonites [12:26–31].

[Transition] We have a great God, do we not? Joy filled my heart this week at the confidence I can have, that you can have, that *God will use us*. We can get so down on ourselves. We can feel like we are the only one we know with our particular struggle. And yet, *God's willingness to use us* is less about which *sins sidetrack* us and more about our willingness to own up to them. To *repent* and return to him.

---

2. For evidence that God is free to "change course" in response to repentance, even after he has made a threat that is worded unconditionally, see Jeremiah 18:7–10, and then note this dynamic at work in God's response to Nineveh in Jonah 3:1, 4–5, 10. Cf. 2 Sam. 12:22.

It is also a good reminder that God is not a doormat. He *disciplines* us. We are his children.

[**BUY**] But some of us may feel, "Ben, I'm glad to know that when I fail to trust God, he will use me to *further his plans*, if I return to him. The problem is, I don't know if I can trust God, if he *disciplines* people the way he disciplined David. That's scary."

Friend, I'm with you. It would be a frightening thing if God *disciplined* everyone like that. The good news is our passage doesn't suggest, doesn't even hint, that God would *discipline* us the same way. In fact, no passage in the Bible does.

David was a unique person in a fairly unique situation at a different stage of God's *plan of salvation*. God sees the big picture, and sometimes he acts in ways that are impossible to understand.

God knows you, too. He knows your unique situation. He cares for you—deeply. He never allows us to be tempted beyond what we can bear, and let me suggest, he'll never *discipline* you beyond what you can bear. That's not God's purpose for *discipline*.

I invite you. Press on. Trust him. This auditorium is full of people who have done just that. God's disciplined all of them. They may not have liked it, but God's never *disciplined* any of them harshly.

[**APPLY**] How might it increase our faithfulness to know that *God will use us to fulfill his plan of salvation, but that sin brings discipline?* Maybe you're a dad who's concerned about how your kids will be able to afford college one day. Imagine:

> Your eyes open. It's Saturday morning. [squinting] "7 am?!" [vocal grogginess turns into an optimistic smile] "Nothing coffee can't fix!" You head to the kitchen, kiss your wife, grab

a cup of joe, and join the kids for breakfast. "You guys ready to play baseball today?" [Kids' reply:] "Of course, Dad."

Two hours later you're driving to your oldest son's baseball game. He's thirteen. You think about college and finances: "The only way he can afford college is if he gets a sports scholarship. He's doing okay, but he's got to improve. He's got to practice more."

The game begins. You notice he's batting seventh. In his first at-bat, he strikes out. On his second at-bat, he grounds out. Ditto on the third. You're frustrated.

After the game, as you head to the car together, you resolve to shoot straight with your son: "He needs to know how this college thing works." You put on a calm smile. You walk right up next to him, so no one else will be able to hear what you're about to say. You adjust your vocal chords, ready to say with a harsh tone, "Why don't you get it? You need to stop goofing around after school and start practicing. College is expensive. If I can't afford it, you can't afford it. You've got to get a baseball scholarship. You wanna go to college, you wanna be somebody, don't you?"

But then the thought arises, "*God will use me to fulfill his plan of salvation, so long as I keep coming back to him, but sin brings discipline.*" You reflect: "If I take the next few years to ruin my relationship with my son over a baseball scholarship, God may still find a way to use me, but what will it cost me? I could lose my son. I could ruin my testimony. I don't want that."

"Lord, all I want is to give my kids a chance to succeed in life, but you're right. I can't do it by provoking my son's anger. You know what's best, and there's no need to invite your *discipline*. Give me wisdom."

As you continue to walk to the car, you relax. Your frustration lessens. As you open the trunk, you look at your son and say, "It was a good game today."

"Dad, it was a terrible game. I never even reached first base. I'm never gonna get a college scholarship."

"Maybe. Maybe not. Let's trust God and see what happens. You don't need a scholarship to be great in God's eyes or mine."

"Thanks, Dad."

I can't tell you whether your son will get a scholarship or not. What I can tell you is that, at that moment, *God used you to fulfill his plan of salvation*. God used you to bring your son closer to Jesus.

We never know what our faithfulness will lead to. You gave your son's teammate a ride home from the game that day. He's a good kid, but he's had a rough life. In ten years, he might see you around town and say, "Do you remember that time you said that no son of yours needs a scholarship to be great in your eyes or God's? When I heard that, I thought, 'If God can make someone into a dad like that, then I need God in my life. Thanks.'"

CONCLUSION
[REVIEW] Friends, we've seen this morning that *God will use us, his ambassadors, to fulfill his plan of salvation, but sin brings discipline.*

[FINAL PUSH] It takes a lot of work. In some cases, a lot of donations to a political party to serve for a few years as a United States *ambassador* to another country. It's a noble position.

Few of us will ever have the chance to become a US ambassador, but all of us here are invited to become an *ambassador of Christ*. No special skills, no money is necessary. Only a willingness to place your faith in Jesus Christ. If you have not yet entered into a full-time faith commitment to Jesus Christ, do so today.

Let's all have confidence this week knowing that *God is using us to fulfill his plans*, to further the gospel. It may not look like it. We may wonder how, but let's have that confidence. Don't hold back. If you've become *sidetracked*, return to the God who embraces you.

[CLOSING AFFIRMATION] I trust you will. Amen.

APPENDIX C

Sermon from Genesis 11:1–9

This sermon was delivered to a men's group at an Armenian congregation in Orange County, CA. Many of them grew up in the Eastern Orthodox Church. I preached from the New International Version, which was chosen to enhance clarity, as it was the translation most in the audience were using. The indentation and labels are retained from the original manuscript.

Words that appear in the THT, or the question it answers, are italicized throughout the manuscript, except when they appear in the Focus or when the THT is "officially" stated in the body of the sermon (see ch. 6).

> **[ENGAGE]** Nikita Khrushchev was president of the Soviet Union after Stalin. His relationship with Armenia was a mixed one.
>
> Khrushchev once asked a child, "Who is your father?"
> The boy replied, "Nikita Khrushchev is my father."
> "And who is your mother?"
> "The Communist Party."
> "Very good. Now tell me, what would you like to be when you grow up?"
> The boy replied [with a broken voice], "I wanna be an orphan."
>
> Like that boy, we all have a vision of who we want to be. We all want to be known for something. To *make a name for ourselves*. That vision, *that name*, may have changed over time. Life throws us curve balls, and we have to adapt.

God gives us a lot of freedom to make decisions. But God warns us to not go too far. Whatever direction our lives are heading—college, business, ministry, retirement—*God calls us to align ourselves with his redemptive plans.* He calls us to live a life that reflects a full-time faith commitment to Jesus Christ.

That's a scary proposition. I see teenagers in here. *Aligning yourself with God's redemptive plans* might mean dropping out of the popular crowd. It might mean leaving the party scene and stopping the pursuit of the ladies. These are life-and-death issues for high school and college students. They were for me. When I came to Christ at seventeen I was giving up everything I had lived my life for.

If *aligning ourselves with God's redemptive plans* is a scary proposition to teenagers, how much more to those of us who are older? The stakes are higher. Many of us work to support spouses, children, even grandchildren. You live in Southern California. Life's expensive.

Piety can seem a bit theoretical. To feed our families and live in a safe community, we need to be successful.

To want to be successful is to be American. To be good at it is to be Armenian. My first pastor, Armenian. My first professor of preaching, Armenian. My mortgage broker, Armenian; he descends from the Agajanian racing family. My friend, your pastor, Shant, Armenian. All of them successful.

Many successful people, however, don't seem to concern themselves with piety, with godliness. When money's on the line, even the most devout among us may struggle to put God's *redemptive plans* first.

Sermon from Genesis 11:1–9

Let's be real. God seems to let us get away with a lot. He may discipline us, but we often don't recognize it for what it is. He calls us to *align ourselves with his redemptive plans*, but we may wonder, "What's the big deal?"

[FOCUS] So then, why should we align ourselves with God's redemptive plans? What's the problem with making a name for ourselves, in defiance of God's plans? Why should we participate actively in what God is doing to establish a people for his name? This morning we're going to look at a passage that answers that question.

[SET THE STAGE] It tells of a time shortly after the Flood. God's plan to bring salvation to the world through Jesus Christ was at an early stage. God gave the people one simple command: Be fruitful, multiply, and fill the earth. Have children, from such children have other children, and spread out. Scatter. Disperse. Keep migrating. Fill the known world with people.

It sounds simple enough, but it cramped their style. They didn't have airplanes. They didn't have cars. The horse and buggy would have been advanced technology to them. The thought of generations of nomadic life wasn't appealing.

[PREVIEW] We're going to look at this narrative together. Appreciate it on its terms. As we do, it'll become clear *why we should align ourselves with God's redemptive plans*.

[ANNOUNCE PASSAGE] Let's open our Bibles to the book of Genesis . . . that amazing first book of the Bible . . . page 10 in the Blue Bibles . . . Genesis chapter 11 . . . Genesis 11.

[MOVEMENT] As the story opens, we find the whole known world—the descendants of Noah—unified by a single language.

They migrate east. Jackpot: Shinar. A perfectly reasonable place to establish permanent residence—*in defiance of God's redemptive plans.*

> [READ] Read with me verses 1 and 2, "¹Now the whole world had one language and a common speech. ²As men moved eastward, they found a plain in Shinar and settled there."
>
> [EXPLAIN] Note, the end of verse 2 says they "settled there." They all wanted to establish permanent residence. Had some settled there and most moved on, no problem. But the entire community decided: "This place is great. Let's make it our home."
>
> Can you blame them? By the ancient world's standards, Shinar was incredible. Sure, they were *defying God's redemptive plans*, but where is God?
>
> It can be hard to sacrifice, to yield our will to God's, when prosperity's at stake. When God's will gets in the way of the *name we're making for ourselves.*

[MOVEMENT] The people's excitement, the benefits of their *defiance* in Shinar, produces a spirit of collegiality and community. "Let's use our finest building materials to build a city-tower," they say to each other. "We can succeed on our own. We'll have stability, power, and success."

> [READ] Read with me verses 3 and 4, "³They said to each other, 'Come, let's make bricks and bake them thoroughly.' They used brick instead of stone, and tar for mortar. ⁴Then they said, 'Come, let us build ourselves a city, with a tower that reaches to the heavens, so that we may make a name for ourselves and not be scattered over the face of the whole earth.'

Sermon from Genesis 11:1–9

[Transition] We have to wonder, "Where is God in all this?" It took the ancient world a long time to build large structures. They couldn't build a local Taco Bell in twenty-four hours, like we can. It could take decades to build towers and temples. God seems absent, as their hubris—their overestimated sense of self-importance—grows daily. If these people—if we in our lives—can get away with our *plans* in *defiance* of God's will, then *why should we align ourselves with his redemptive plans? Why not make a name for ourselves,* if God will let us get away with it?

[LEAD-IN] It's at this point we're given a heavy dose of reality and a good measure of sarcasm.

> [READ] Look at verse 5, "⁵But the Lord came down to see the city and the tower that the men were building."
>
> [EXPLAIN] Here the people are, here are so many today, *defying God's redemptive plans*, and thinking, "Where is your God?" Verse 5 hits us with a steady dose of reality: God is watching. He sees what we're doing. Make no mistake about it.
>
> Verse 5 also hits us with a good measure of sarcasm. The people were so proud of themselves: "Who else can build a tower that reaches into the heavens?" Yet verse 5 says the Lord had to come way down just to see what they're doing.
>
> The picture, here, is of God sitting atop his lofty perch [stand on a chair]. It's as if God is saying, "Hey angels, I hear the folks at Shinar think they've got things figured out. I hear they're building a tower that'll reach way up into the sky. Do you see anything?" The angels reply, "You mean [squinting eyes and pointing down, as if trying to identify a speck of dust from a distance] right there. I think I see something." God replies, "That's it, right down there. I'm going to check it out."

[**Transition**] As God, metaphorically, makes the long trek down, the Bible tells us we reach a pivotal point in human history. God must choose: Let the people *thwart his redemptive plans* or continue *his redemptive plans by thwarting their plans*. God chooses redemption. Friends, we have a God whose nature doesn't allow him to abandon *his redemptive plans*. His plans can't be thwarted.

In the verses we are about to read, it becomes clear *why we must align ourselves with God's redemptive plans*. We discover *the problem with making a name for ourselves, in defiance of God's plans*.

[**THT**] We should align ourselves with God's redemptive plans, because God's redemptive plans will prevail. It's futile to make a name for ourselves, because God will ultimately thwart our efforts.

[**MOVEMENT**] This becomes clear as God responds to the people's *defiance* by giving them new languages.

> [**READ**] Let's read, beginning at verse 6, "⁶The Lord said, 'If as one people speaking the same language they have begun to do this, then nothing they plan to do will be impossible for them. ⁷Come, let us go down and confuse their language so they will not understand each other."

[**MOVEMENT**] The Lord's word comes true. The building stops. *God's redemptive plans prevail*, as the people disperse. They continue to fill the whole known world. In an ironic twist, the inhabitants of Shinar are given *a name*: Babel, meaning confusion:

> [**READ**] Read with me verses 8 and 9, "⁸So the Lord scattered them from there over all the earth, and they stopped building the city. ⁹That is why it was called Babel—because there the Lord confused the language of the whole world. From there the Lord scattered them over the face of the whole earth."

[Transition] That *God's redemptive plans will prevail* has significant consequences for all of us.

For one, if we ignore them, there will come a day when we realize that our greatest accomplishments, *the name we've made for ourselves*, the things we pride ourselves on the most, will be our undoing.

We live at a different stage in God's *plans*. It's no longer God's central concern to fill the earth. At seven billion people, that requirement has been fulfilled. That was an early stage.

God went on. He established a covenant with Abraham. Through Abraham came the nation Israel. From Israel was born Jesus Christ, who lived the perfect life in our place, died on the cross for our sins, and rose again from the dead.

[APPLY] In our context, what can we do now that we've seen that *God's redemptive plans will prevail?*

> Maybe you're a little like me. I grew up in a more formal church environment. I've always been pro-church. If you'd've asked me if I believed in God, I would have said, "Yes." If you'd've asked me if I believed in "Jesus," I would have said, "Definitely."
>
> I went to church from time to time. I knew I wasn't following God too closely, but I was pretty sure I was good enough. I would have been upset if someone suggested I didn't have "biblical faith."
>
> That changed one night. I was in my room alone. I opened the Bible. I began to read Jesus' words. I had never read the Bible on my own. Jesus was clear: God's call to *align ourselves with his redemptive plans* is non-negotiable. I must enter into a full-time faith commitment to Jesus Christ.

If you have not done that, do what I did. Make that decision. Place your faith in Jesus Christ. Enter into a full-time faith commitment to Jesus Christ. Admit to God you have been *defying his redemptive plans*. You've been going your own way, and you want to join the winning team. We ignore his call at our own peril.

God wants this passage to strengthen the faith of even the most faithful among us.

Maybe you're a retired businessman. What can you do to more fully *align yourself with God's redemptive plans*? Consider growing your relationship with your adult children.

> The reality is that many of us have adult children whose faith is weak or nonexistent, and it stems from decades-old parent-child tensions.
>
> Dads, your adult children are still trying to impress you. They still want you to delight in them. Even billionaire Ted Turner admitted that recently—and his dad passed away decades ago.
>
> Give your kids a call. Invite them over to the house for lunch, one-on-one. If they live across the county, fly out to see them.
>
> Be vulnerable. Share with them. If your son or daughter feels—or has suppressed feelings—that you spent too much time at work and not enough with them growing up, share with 'em, "Hey, I wanted to get together with you today to say sorry for not valuing time with you like I should have when you were growing up. I want you to know: I delight in you more than I can express. When you were growing up I was too caught up trying to make it in this world."

Of course, don't stop at that conversation. Commit yourself to developing a deep, vulnerable, non-defensive relationship with them.

I can't tell you how they'll respond. Humans are unpredictable. Your son might break down and cry. Your daughter might launch into a tirade of everything she's still hurt by.

What I can tell you is the more you develop a deep, vulnerable relationship with them, the more you are *aligning yourself with God's redemptive plans.* The more you are participating in his plan to bring people to himself.

And who knows, you may find that because you took those steps, the faith will be strong in your family for generations.

CONCLUSION
[**REVIEW**] Friends, there is great news: God wins. *We should align ourselves with his redemptive plans because his redemptive plans will prevail. It's futile to make a name for ourselves, because God will ultimately thwart our efforts.*

[**FINAL PUSH**] Be successful. That's great. You're Armenians! Yet may God *name* you and your family among the faithful to Jesus Christ. Embrace him fully.

[**CLOSING AFFIRMATION**] I trust you will. Amen.

APPENDIX D

Storyline of the Old Testament

What follows is an overview of the OT's storyline. Its purpose is to provide an easily understandable way for us to sense the unfolding plan of God in the OT. Many preachers admit in private conversation their struggle to understand the storyline of the OT. They've heard the parts, but can't put them together. Naturally, it can be difficult to understand what's going on in the OT, if we can't see the big picture.

ADAM (& EVE)
Story Line: Gen. 2–4
pre-Old Covenant: Gen. 3:15
↓

SETH
Story Line: Gen. 4–5
↓

NOAH
Story Line: Gen. 6–9
pre-Old Covenant: Gen. 9:1–17
↓

ABRAHAM
Story Line: Gen. 12–25
Old Covenant: Gen. 12:1–3
Old Covenant Expansion: Gen. 15 (Promised Land)
Old Covenant Expansion: Gen. 17 (Circumcision)
Well-Known People: Abraham, Sarah, Isaac
↓

ISAAC
STORY LINE: GEN. 21–28
WELL-KNOWN PEOPLE: ISAAC, REBEKAH, ESAU, JACOB
↓
JACOB (renamed ISRAEL)
STORY LINE: GEN. 25–35; 46–49
WELL-KNOWN PEOPLE: JACOB/ISRAEL, LEAH, RACHEL
↓
TWELVE SONS/TRIBES OF ISRAEL
STORY LINE: GEN. 25–50
WELL-KNOWN PEOPLE: JOSEPH, JUDAH, LEVI
↓
MOSES
LEADS ISRAEL UP TO PROMISED LAND
STORY LINE: EXODUS, NUMBERS, DEUTERONOMY
OLD COVENANT EXPANSION: EXOD. 19:1–5; 20;
ALL OF DEUT., ESP. 1:7–8; 7:7–10; 9:4–6; 28 (LAW)
WELL-KNOWN PEOPLE: MOSES, AARON, PHARAOH, CALEB

MAJOR EVENTS:
TEN PLAGUES (EXOD. 7–12); PASSOVER (EXOD. 12);
TEN COMMANDMENTS (EXOD. 20; DEUT. 5);
ARK OF THE COVENANT (EXOD. 25; 37);
TABERNACLE/TENT OF MEETING (EXOD. 26; 35; 40)
↓
JOSHUA
LEADS ISRAEL INTO THE PROMISED LAND
STORY LINE: JOSHUA
WELL-KNOWN PEOPLE: JOSHUA, RAHAB, CALEB

MAJOR EVENTS:
THE CONQUEST (JOSH. 5–13); FALL OF JERICHO (JOSH. 6)
↓

JUDGES RULE ISRAEL
Story Line: Judges; Ruth
Well-Known People: Gideon, Samson, Ruth, Boaz
↓
UNITED KINGDOM/MONARCHY
ONE KING RULES ALL TWELVE TRIBES OF ISRAEL
Story Line: 1–2 Sam.; 1 Kings 1–11; 1 Chron.; 2 Chron. 1–9
Time Period: 1051–1011 BC

Well-Known People: Samuel, King Saul,
King David, King Solomon
Major Event: (First/Solomon's) Temple Built (1 Kings 5–7)
↓
DIVIDED KINGDOM/MONARCHY
ISRAEL SPLITS INTO TWO SEPARATE KINGDOMS
Story Line: 1 Kings 12; 2 Chron. 10
Time Period: 931 BC

SOUTHERN KINGDOM (JUDAH)	**NORTHERN KINGDOM (ISRAEL)**
Later known as Jews	**Later known as Samaritans**
Formed from the tribes of Judah and Benjamin	Formed from the other ten tribes
↓	↓
RULED BY VARIOUS KINGS FROM THE LINE OF DAVID	**RULED BY VARIOUS KINGS AND SET UP OWN HYBRID RELIGION**
Story Line: 1 Kings 13–22; 2 Kings 1–17; 18–25; 2 Chron. 11–36	Story Line: 1 Kings 13–22; 2 Kings 1–17
Well-Known People: King Jeroboam, King Ahab, Elijah, Elisha, Naaman
↓

TIME PERIOD: 931–597 BC
WELL-KNOWN PEOPLE:
KING ASA, KING AHAZ, KING HEZEKIAH, ISAIAH, JEREMIAH, KING JOSIAH
↓
EXILE
Taken Captive/Deported by Babylonians
STORY LINE: DANIEL
TIME PERIOD: 597–538 BC
WELL-KNOWN PEOPLE:
DANIEL, SHADRACH, MESHACH, ABEDNEGO, NEBUCHADNEZZAR
↓
**RETURN FROM EXILE
&
TEMPLE REBUILT**
(aka Second Temple)
STORY LINE: EZRA
TIME PERIOD: 538–458 BC
WELL-KNOWN PEOPLE:
EZRA, CYRUS (KING OF PERSIA)
↓
**JERUSALEM REBUILT
&
SOCIAL RELIGIOUS REFORMS**
STORY LINE: NEHEMIAH
WELL-KNOWN PEOPLE:
NEHEMIAH, EZRA
↓

**TAKEN CAPTIVE BY ASSYRIANS
&
INTERMARRY w/ OTHER GROUPS**
↓
Less than one thousand Samaritans today (est.)

Storyline of the Old Testament

AFTER OLD TESTAMENT UNTIL CHRIST
(Intertestamental Period)
Persian Empire Controls Jerusalem
TIME PERIOD: 430–332 BC

MAJOR EVENTS:
PERSIAN EMPIRE CONTINUES REIGN AS WORLD POWER
↓

Greek Empire Controls Jerusalem
TIME PERIOD: 331–167 BC

MAJOR EVENTS:
- Roman Empire conquers Jerusalem and Middle East by 331 BC

- "Hellenization": Conquered cultures adopt Greek language and culture

- Antiochus Epiphanes desecrates Jewish Temple by sacrificing pig on altar; kills 100,000 Jews

WELL-KNOWN PEOPLE:
ALEXANDER THE GREAT, ANTIOCHUS EPIPHANES
↓

Jews Control Jerusalem
TIME PERIOD: 167–63 BC

MAJOR EVENTS
- Maccabean revolt successful in response to the persecution of Antiochus Epiphanes

- Jewish independence under Hasmonean rule

- Hanukkah established, which celebrates the cleansing and rededication of the Temple after Judas Maccabeus gained independence from Antiochus Epiphanes/Greek Empire

WELL-KNOWN PEOPLE:
JUDAS MACCABEUS,
JOHN HYRCANUS
↓

Roman Empire Controls Jerusalem
TIME PERIOD:
63 BC–LIFE OF CHRIST

MAJOR EVENTS
- Roman Empire conquers the Greek Empire and also Palestine (which includes the region of Judea and the city of Jerusalem)

- Roman Empire puts Herod the Great in charge of Palestine (a non-Jewish Edomite)

- Herod the Great initiates the reconstruction of the four-hundred-year-old Second Temple, which was in its forty-sixth year of construction in 27 AD

- Five groups emerge within Judaism: Sadducees, Pharisees, Zealots, Essenes, and the common people. Most Jews were common people, who were not members of the other four groups and who were criticized by the rabbis for the lack of religious practice.

- After Herod the Great died, the Jews' relationship with the Roman Empire went sour. The province of Judea was broken into four sections, with each ruled by a "governor." By 70 AD, war broke out between them, and Jerusalem was destroyed.

WELL-KNOWN PEOPLE:
HEROD THE GREAT,
SADDUCEES, PHARISEES,
ZEALOTS, ESSENES,
COMMON PEOPLE

Bibliography

Amit, Yaira. *Reading Biblical Narratives: Literary Criticism and the Hebrew Bible*. Minneapolis: Fortress, 2001.

Arthurs, Jeffrey, and Andrew Gurevich. "Theological and Rhetorical Perspectives on Self-Disclosure in Preaching." *Bibliotheca Sacra* 157, April–June (2000): 215–26.

Bar-Efrat, Shimeon. *Narrative Art in the Bible*. Sheffield: Almond, 1989.

Bauer, Walter, Frederick W. Danker, F. W. Gingrich, and William F. Arndt. *A Greek-English Lexicon of the New Testament and Other Early Christian Literature*. 3rd ed. Chicago: University of Chicago, 2000.

Beale, G. K., and D. A. Carson, eds. *Commentary on the New Testament Use of the Old Testament*. Grand Rapids: Baker, 2007.

Blomberg, Craig L. *Matthew*. New American Commentary. Nashville: Broadman, 1992.

Buis, Harry. "Retribution." *Zondervan Encyclopedia of the Bible*. Edited by Merrill C. Tenney and Moisés Silva. Revised Full-Color Edition, vol. 5. Grand Rapids: Zondervan, 2009.

Catechism of the Catholic Church. Vatican City: Libreria Editrice Vaticana, 1994.

Chapell, Bryan. *Christ-Centered Preaching: Redeeming the Expository Sermon*. 2nd ed. Grand Rapids: Baker, 2005.

Chisholm, Robert B. *Interpreting the Historical Books: An Exegetical Handbook*. Grand Rapids: Kregel, 2006.

Dallaire, Hélène. "Judaism and the World to Come." In *A Case for Historic Premillenialism: An Alternative to "Left Behind" Eschatology*, edited by Craig L. Blomberg and Sung Wook Chung, 37–60. Grand Rapids: Baker, 2009.

Danker, Frederick William. *The Concise Greek-English Lexicon of the New Testament*. Chicago: University of Chicago, 2009.

Dunn-Wilson, David. *A Mirror for the Church: Preaching in the First Five Centuries*. Grand Rapids: Eerdmans, 2005.

Featherstone, James. "Evaluating the Effectiveness of Five Forms of Expositional Preaching with the Four Active Generations of Church Membership." In *2009 EHS Conference Papers*, 1–13. Proceedings of Promoting Community through Preaching, Southwestern Baptist Theological Seminary, Fort Worth, TX. http://ehomiletics.com/members

Fee, Gordon D. *The First Epistle to the Corinthians*. New International Commentary on the New Testament. 2nd ed. Grand Rapids: Eerdmans, 2014.

Fee, Gordon D., and Douglas K. Stuart. *How to Read the Bible for All Its Worth*. 4th ed. Grand Rapids: Zondervan, 2014.

Firth, David G. *1 & 2 Samuel*. Apollos Old Testament Commentary. Nottingham: Apollos, 2009.

Greidanus, Sidney. *The Modern Preacher and the Ancient Text: Interpreting and Preaching Biblical Literature*. Grand Rapids: Eerdmans, 1988.

_____. "The Necessity of Preaching Christ Also from Old Testament Texts." *Calvin Theological Journal* 34 (1999): 188–97.

_____. *Preaching Christ from Genesis*. Grand Rapids: Eerdmans, 2007.

_____. *Preaching Christ from Daniel*. Grand Rapids: Eerdmans, 2012.

Harmon-Jones, Eddie. "Cognitive Dissonance." *Encyclopedia of the Mind*. Edited by Harold Pashler. Vol. 1. Los Angeles: Sage, 2013.

Hill, Andrew E., and John H. Walton. *A Survey of the Old Testament*. 3rd ed. Grand Rapids: Zondervan, 2009.

Hooke, Ruthanna B. "Humor in Preaching: Life Touched by Grace." *Word & World* 32, no. 2 (Spring 2012): 187–89.

Jacks, Robert. *Just Say the Word!: Writing for the Ear*. Grand Rapids: Eerdmans, 1996.

Keener, Craig S. *A Commentary on the Gospel of Matthew*. Grand Rapids: Eerdmans, 1999.

Klein, William W., Craig Blomberg, and Robert L. Hubbard. *Introduction to Biblical Interpretation*. Rev. and Exp. ed. Dallas: Word, 2004.

Kuruvilla, Abraham. *Privilege the Text!: A Theological Hermeneutic for Preaching*. Chicago: Moody, 2013.

Longman III, Tremper. *Literary Approaches to Biblical Interpretation*. Grand Rapids: Zondervan, 1987.

Mathewson, Steven D. *The Art of Preaching Old Testament Narrative*. Grand Rapids: Baker, 2002.

Mathison, Keith A. *The Shape of Sola Scriptura*. Moscow, ID: Canon Press, 2001.

Matthews, Bo. "He Who Has Ears to Hear ... Jeremiah 1." In *Biblical Sermons: How Twelve Preachers Apply the Principles of Biblical Preaching*, edited by Haddon W. Robinson, 113–32. Grand Rapids: Baker, 1989.

Monroe, Alan, Douglas Ehninger, and Bruce Gronbeck. *Principles and Types of Speech Communication*. 8th ed. Glenview, IL: Scott, Foresman, 1978.

Osborne, Grant R. *The Hermeneutical Spiral: A Comprehensive Introduction to Biblical Interpretation*. Rev. and Expanded ed. Downers Grove, IL: InterVarsity, 2006.

Piper, John. *The Supremacy of God in Preaching*. Grand Rapids: Baker, 1990.

Robinson, Haddon W. *Biblical Preaching: The Development and Delivery of Expository Messages*. 3rd ed. Grand Rapids: Baker, 2014.

———. "The Heresy of Application." In *The Art and Craft of Biblical Preaching*, edited by Haddon W. Robinson and Craig Brian Larson, 998–99. Grand Rapids: Zondervan, 2005.

Shore, Mary Hinkle. "Leave Them Wanting More: Humor in Preaching." *Word & World* 32, no. 2 (Spring 2012): 124–31.

Stibbs, Alan M. *Expounding God's Word: Some Principles and Methods*. Grand Rapids: Eerdmans, 1960.

Stuart, Douglas K. *Exodus*. New American Commentary. Nashville: Broadman & Holman, 2006.

———. *Old Testament Exegesis: A Handbook for Students and Pastors.* 4th ed. Louisville: Westminster John Knox, 2009.

Sunukjian, Donald R. "The Credibility of the Preacher." *Bibliotheca Sacra*, July–September (1982): 255–66.

———. *Invitation to Biblical Preaching: Proclaiming Truth with Clarity and Relevance.* Grand Rapids: Kregel, 2007.

———. "The Preacher as Persuader." In *Walvoord: A Tribute*, edited by Donald K. Campbell, 289–99. Chicago: Moody, 1982.

Thiselton, Anthony C. *The First Epistle to the Corinthians.* New International Greek Testament Commentary. Grand Rapids: Eerdmans, 2000.

Vogt, Peter T. *Interpreting the Pentateuch: An Exegetical Handbook.* Grand Rapids: Kregel, 2009.

Walton, Ben. "Philosophical Hermeneutics and Evangelical Preaching." In *2014 EHS Conference Papers.* Proceedings of Hermeneutics for Homiletics, Moody Bible Institute, Chicago. http://ehomiletics.com/members

Walton, John H., and Andrew E. Hill. *Old Testament Today: A Journey from Ancient Context to Contemporary Relevance.* 2nd ed. Grand Rapids: Zondervan, 2014.

Walton, John H. "Retribution." In *Dictionary of the Old Testament: Wisdom, Poetry & Writings*, edited by Tremper Longman III and Peter Enns, 647–55. Downers Grove, IL: InterVarsity, 2008.

Warren, Paul Christopher. "By What Authority? Pitfalls in Pulpit Interpretation." *Interpretation* 1 (April 1947): 207–18.

Wenham, Gordon J. *Story as Torah: Reading Old Testament Narrative Ethically.* Grand Rapids: Baker, 2004.

Wilson, Paul Scott. *Preaching and Homiletical Theory.* St. Louis: Chalice Press, 2004.

Youngblood, Ronald F. "2 Samuel." In *1 Samuel–2 Kings*, edited by Tremper Longman III and David E. Garland. Rev. ed., vol. 3. Expositor's Bible Commentary. Grand Rapids: Zondervan, 2009.

About the Author

Benjamin H. Walton (D.Min., Gordon-Conwell Theological Seminary) is president of PreachingWorks, an organization dedicated to helping pastors maximize their preaching potential. A former pastor, Ben has taught courses or lectured at several schools including Grand Canyon University, Arizona Christian University, and Talbot School of Theology.